LOCKED
IN
TIME

I Still Remember And Always Will

BONNIE J. TIERNEY

Outskirts Press, Inc.
Denver, Colorado

Outskirts Press
http://www.outskirtspress.com

ISBN-13: 978-1-4327-0726-2

Library of Congress Control Number: 2007928005

Outskirts Press and the "OP" logo are trademarks belonging to Outskirts Press, Inc.

Printed in the United States of America

TABLE OF CONTENTS

Dedication V
Acknowledgements VII

The Beginning 1

My Trip To Pikes Peak 7

The Call To Duty 13

The Love In My Heart 33

The Two French Soldiers 39

Homeland Insecurity 47

Keeping Good Company 51

Tears Keep Coming 57

My Paper To Congress 63

On My Political SoapBox 75

Grace 85

Get On With Your Life 125

I Still Remember 133

My Uncle Jake – My Hero..139

Another Trip Down Memory Lane 147

The VA Red Tape 159

My Wish For America 173

Dedicated to the 241 Marines, who lost their lives as a result of the tragic bombing of the Marine Barracks in Beirut, Lebanon, on October 23, 1983, while serving as Peace Keepers and to my son, Staff Sergeant Jason Paul Caceres, who is currently serving in Iraq.

ACKNOWLEDGEMENTS

I want to thank my son, Staff Sergeant Jason Paul Caceres, who has made me very proud of his accomplishments over the years. He continues to make me laugh and gives me complete reason to live. While he is stationed in the very country where I first became "Locked In Time," serving on active duty with the United States Air Force, I pray that he will be safe from harm and will never have to witness the atrocities of senseless terrorist acts as I did 24 years earlier. I am not blind though, with the proposed escalation of troops moving into Iraq that my only son could be deployed any day to support the President's mission. It will be music to my ears to hear the real "Mission Accomplished." (It's 11:15 a.m., January 28, 2007, Colorado time) – and I just received a call from my son, Jason. He has received his orders to participate in the Iraq War and will be going to Baghdad late April. Who could imagine within minutes of writing my acknowledgement to him that I would receive a call telling me this bad news?

I owe my deepest gratitude to my sister, Karen Tierney, for loving me in every way and for providing me a home when I was homeless. If it were not for my sister's encouragement to seek psychiatric treatment for my Post Traumatic Stress Disorder (PTSD), I may have continued to be "Locked In Time." It helps to have a nurse for a sister and I must say, she is a remarkable nurse too. She followed in my maternal grandmother's footsteps and is truly one of the most caring and loving people I've ever known. My younger sister, Robin Meredith, certainly listened to many of my stories over the years, listened to my hardships and to my desperate cry for help. Although misinterpreted over the years, she finally experienced a revelation to understand that the state of my mental health was not a result of being in love with someone I have known for years, but rather associated with my own nightmare I experienced while serving on active duty with the United States Air Force. My direct involvement with the recovery, identification and processing of the 241 Marines who were killed in Beirut, Lebanon, during the bombing of the Marine Barracks on October 23, 1983, was something I could have never imagined and my sister Robin has always been there for me and I love her greatly. The eldest sometimes gets over looked and coming from a family of four, the first-born was my brother, Tom Tierney. He currently lives in California with his wife, Linda. Each of my siblings served on active duty with my brother being the first to join the military at the early age of 17. He served during the Vietnam conflict and I'm proud of his service to our country. I'm sure that my brother also suffers from long term PTSD, but he may not even recognize it as such. If he did, he would never admit to it. Over the years, he's managed to numb his pain by a gambling addiction. I understand that pain and I understand addictive behavior. Whether it's drinking, being in and out of relationships, having sexual encounters or going on spending sprees; it is associated with the effects of PTSD. He manages his anxiety and his obsessive-compulsive disorder (OCD) the same way I have, by taking lots of meds. We are a proud family and although my parents, Jacob and Myrtle Tierney are deceased, they would be extremely proud.

I could not even begin to finish this book without thanking Kay Jared for her love, compassion and support she provided me through my very tumultuous years after I left the military on September 11, 1992. She was a steady rock in my life and offered me her home and taught me the importance of living in the here and now. She suffered greatly as a result of my personal struggles with PTSD. Any spouse, partner or family member suffers greatly when living with someone who has PTSD. I only wished that I had sought treatment much earlier in my relationship with Kay because it would have made a big difference, not only for me, but also for her. I would also like to thank Kay for proofreading my manuscript and providing me invaluable feedback.

Today, I am working with the Department of Veterans Affairs as an Administrative Officer for the Facilities Management Service. The direction of my life has changed significantly and I must thank Ms. Marcie Sardinta, Mr. James Anderson, Ms. Connie Drake and Mr. Bradley McCollam, the Chief of Facilities Management for hiring me. As I mentioned to Brad on many occasions, I would have been living out of my car or maybe wouldn't be here today if it were not for the team's decision to hire me.

There is a great need today, to reach out to our female veterans and offer them counseling for many different reasons. Women veterans are still the silent minority and unlike the Vietnam nurses who went silently home to live the remainder of their lives, most without counseling, most without treatment from the VA, our younger and more recent female veterans are beginning to seek help. There is no shame in admitting you need help.

To my military brothers and sisters serving on active duty or to those who have served in combat related activities, don't wait until you are in that deep tunnel, to ask for help. I repeat again, there is no shame in admitting you need help. If my experiences send you running to the mental health counselors, then I will have achieved my goal for writing this book. I intend to donate the royalties (profits) derived from "Locked in Time" to the mental health program, Department of Veterans Affairs, Denver, Colorado, for the care of veterans with PTSD. May I make millions – and give it all back – for I would not be alive today if it were not for the caring staff!

CHAPTER 1
THE BEGINNING

I first began writing my memoirs while I was assigned to Eaker Air Force Base in Blytheville, Arkansas, in 1987. I had kept copious notes from my military career, beginning with my enlistment on active duty on October 4, 1973. Somewhere between documenting my writings in 1987 until the time I moved in with my former partner after leaving the military on September 11, 1992, I lost my manuscript and all my notes. Then in December 2000, just after I left my former partner of ten years, I decided to write again. Somewhere between 2000 and 2004, I managed to screw up my life in such a way that I ended up in the lock down psychiatric ward of the Denver Veterans Administration (VA) hospital. I guess that was the best thing that ever happened to me, next to giving birth to my son, Jason, and meeting my current partner, who must remain anonymous for obvious reasons. I'm here now writing the third manuscript to my book. Neither you nor I will ever get to see the first and second edition in print because another former lover, whom I met on match "monster" dot com managed to erase the entire data on my computer. It would be absolutely wonderful if I could erase the memories of that very brief period of my life as quickly as she deleted all my files, but unfortunately I can't. Now that you know I have been involved in too many relationships to count, (one of the many symptoms of Post Traumatic Stress Disorder) there are a lot of people waiting to read "Locked in Time."

Many people have encouraged me through the years to write about my military experiences; however, I never quite knew where to begin. Now, after losing my first and second manuscripts, I decided to…as Nike says, "Just do it." It's April 5, 2005, and I am in my rental room in Aurora, Colorado, lying in my bed. I have no idea how long it will take to write about my military experiences, but I trust it won't take as long as the 19 years I spent on active duty.

The news tonight – Peter Jennings has lung cancer. Now that's a story! I empathize with Peter and lord help him if he has to have a lung removed. I remember the pain both my parents experienced after their lung removal operations. The day my mother came out of the operating room, I swore if I ever got lung cancer, I would never have that operation. The doctors told us having a lung operation is about the most painful operation anyone can undergo. Judging from the look on my mother's face, I would definitely say they were right. Good luck Peter! (I completed my book and as I reflect back and edit my materials, poor Peter Jennings died on August 7, 2005, just four months after he had announced he had lung cancer.)

My own parents, Jacob and Myrtle Tierney, died of lung cancer six months apart from each other. My father was buried on November 18, 1991, and my mother passed away on May 18, 1992. My father was 65 and my mother was 62. They were too young to pass on but being very heavy smokers nearly all their lives, it had to be inevitable. When I was a young child, my entire family would pile into our Pontiac Bonneville and head off to the drive-in theater on Route 5, in South Windsor, Connecticut. We considered going to the drive-in theater in the early 60's our family outing. I would be willing to bet many families considered it their family outing as well. Of course, we were very poor growing up so my father tried to save a few dollars by sneaking me in. My older sister, Karen, and my older brother, Tom, would cover me up in a blanket and throw me on the floorboard and tell me to be quiet as they passed through to pay the drive-in teller. Hiding me on the floorboard was a minor issue compared to my being subjected to secondary smoke from three chain-smokers. Once my father affixed the voice control box to the car window, my older brother and parents would light up their cigarettes. Imagine sitting in a car, windows closed, with three people puffing away. The very minute they lit their cigarettes; the smoke would be so heavy they had to wipe the windshield to see the movie. I usually managed to get out of the car as quickly as possible, making up some excuse the car was too hot and I couldn't breath. Sometimes, I would stick my head out the window whenever my mother rolled her window down. On one occasion, my mother wasn't paying attention and she rolled the window up and my head got stuck and I began choking. Instead of trying to roll the window down, she panicked and tightened the window more. Sticking my head out the window was no longer an option.

I grew up in the projects, on Michael Avenue, East Hartford, Connecticut. I had earaches, soar throats and a horrible sinus condition for most of my entire childhood years. My mother always blamed my condition on Connecticut weather. It wasn't until I arrived in San Antonio, Texas, after enlisting in the Air Force, that I realized the smoke was nearly killing me, not Connecticut weather. I coughed and hacked all the time at home; but as I stayed away from smoke, my lungs began to clear up. It took nearly ten years for my condition to improve and to this day, I still have problems breathing.

Growing up in the projects in East Hartford, Connecticut, was not very easy. My mother was very ill during my childhood and spent many years in an out of Norwich State Hospital. My father worked two jobs just to make ends meet. I prefer not to go too deeply into my early years because it is too painful. Things I remember should never have happened and certainly not to a child and most certainly, not to me. For many years I called it my family "secret," but you would know it as child abuse. Unimaginable actually. My abusers were my brother, father and maternal grandfather and the remote possibility a female family member also abused me, but that memory is very obscure.

Since my mother spent significant time in the hospital, we would visit her on weekends. The hospital was located in New London, Connecticut, and was known as the "State's mental institution." My older brother and sister never liked visiting my mother at the institution and I never understood why in my earlier years. Typically, my father and I would spend time with my mother on the outside grounds. I always enjoyed seeing her. Over the years, I think she spent a good eight or nine years in and out of the hospital and for very long periods. Each time my parents got together, my mother would fight with my father and the doctors would come out to the family picnic center and "haul" her off, sometimes in a straight jacket, and I would be left to see my father in tears. He cried most of the time and it was sad for me to see him cry. I understood many years later why my sister and brother chose not to visit.

To give you a scenario of our very dysfunctional family, I remember one day I was playing in the streets with a group of kids when I heard a loud siren and saw an ambulance heading toward the entryway to our project. As I ran closer to see what was happening, a thick crowd gathered around our apartment. The crowds grew larger in size as I tried to make my way through all the people. When you are a small child surrounded by adults, it's not easy making your way through crowds. I believe I was about six or seven years old at the time. Suddenly, I heard yelling and screaming and the voice sounded much like my mother. I pushed harder to get through the crowds and that's when I saw several men in white coats and my mother strapped down on a gurney. She was screaming, "Where are my children?" The medical team put my mother in a "straight jacket" and before I knew it, they were shoving her inside the ambulance, slamming the door shut only to drive off with the sirens screaming. I chased that ambulance all the way out the driveway, down the street and out of the projects. The crowds broke up and as I started to walk back to our apartment, I saw my father sitting on the front porch. His head hanging, with both hands cupped over his eyes, he sobbed. I recall sitting next to him on the cold cement and laying my head against his shoulder. All I could do is sit and watch him cry. I saw this scenario too many times to count or even remember. To this day, I still have dreams about chasing the ambulance.

CHAPTER 2

MY TRIP TO PIKES PEAK

You probably want to know why I ended up in the Denver Veteran's Administration hospital.

It was May 30, 2004, and I had been watching the Memorial Day round-the-clock news coverage of the World War II memorial dedication in Washington, D.C. The entire week was dedicated to honoring many World War II veterans. The day prior, I had taken a drive from Littleton, Colorado, heading toward Pikes Peak. I was driving my Honda S2000 and had taken my sister's longhaired dachshund, Lady, with me. I hadn't planned on returning to my sister's house. In fact, I hadn't planned anything but driving my car off Pikes Peak.

Watching those World War II veterans was too much stimulation for my mind. Sitting in front of the television, listening to the older generation talk about their painful experiences while serving on active duty, watching all the men cry about the heavy burden each carried as a result of their service to our country, simply overwhelmed me. I internalized their pain and my own grief became too much to handle. After all, a few years earlier, I had walked away from a ten year relationship with someone I loved very much; and then got involved with a monster and abusive woman simply because I was impulsive and didn't want to be alone. Most of all, I was going through my own haunting memories from my experiences in the Air Force and all these circumstances combined, drove me to the point where I felt hopeless and all I could think about was taking my life.

My morning ritual after my sister and her partner left for work was turning on the television to watch the different news channels. I would typically flip back and forth from CNN to Fox News channel and then back to CNN. I often watched CNN because the reporters always seem to cover the best news stories. Please know that people who are living with PTSD should never watch the news, in fact, they should avoid it whenever possible. Television news can be destructive, especially for our veterans. Many veterans who have experienced war tend to get drawn in to watching war movies, or bad news. We tend to get sucked in – like a hurricane or tornado that sucks up metal.

Day after day, I was watching the news about Iraq and listening to the commentators talk about terrorism and death. I was overwhelmed. The more I listened the deeper I internalized everything. I had flash backs from my own military experiences. My thoughts raced. As I listened intently, I internalized the soldiers' pain. They were heart wrenching war stories about their experiences and I got sucked in. Listening to my younger military brothers and sisters' talk about their experiences was also traumatic. I knew what each of them would experience years later. God help them I thought. They too, will spend a life remembering, closing out everyone and everything, being angry with the government, living reckless lives because being self-destructive feels better than being numb. To feel anything at all is something. I jumped in my car, took the dog and just drove south. As I kept driving I kept thinking, "How did I get myself to this point?" I kept telling myself no one would miss me if I drove my car off Pikes Peak, not even my son, Jason. No one would know, but then I looked over at Lady and I thought, how could I take her with me? She's innocent, she didn't ask for this. My mind kept racing and I thought, I'll write a note, tape it to lady and let her go and then drive my car to the top of Pikes Peak and over the edge. I would take the ride of my life…in fact, to the end of my life. It's not that easy though when you have to leave behind people you love. People who really commit suicide are desperate for help and rarely do they ask for help. At one point, when I was close to turning off the road to go up to Pikes Peak, I began sobbing to the point I thought it was raining outside. My tears were just flowing and flowing. I prayed to God to help me. Dear God – help me find the courage to live, to survive and give me the strength that I needed to endure the pain I have felt nearly all of my life.

I was in the right hand lane when all of a sudden a man drove a red VW bug right next to my car. We were riding side by side and he turned his head to look at me, and I swear, he looked like Santa Claus. He had a long white beard and long white hair and he saw me crying. As I wiped my eyes, I felt embarrassed that someone would see me. After all, I was an Air Force officer and I was supposed to "keep my military bearing" and not cry. I was supposed to be tough, at least that's what I believed for most of my 19 years in the military. Okay, so I pinched myself – did I just see Santa Claus? I wiped my eyes again and he was still driving at the same speed I was driving. He began to speed up. He passed me on I-25, just enough to stay ahead of me. As Santa passed, his license plate read, "HO HO 1" and then on the back bumper was a sticker that read, "Miracles happen everyday, remember Christmas."

God sent Santa Claus that day and he was as real as any Santa would be. I'm not crazy because one day, I'm going to thank that man for driving next to me. I never turned up the mountain and in fact, I drove down toward Pueblo, Colorado, and just before I came to Pueblo, there was Santa's village on the left hand side of the road. I know that man lives there now and I haven't been back to look him up, but I can assure you his timing was never better. I'm thankful God sent him that day. I drove about another 20 miles and then turned around and headed back to Littleton. When I got home that evening, I sat down at the supper table and never mentioned a word to my sister. I never told her about that drive until the following morning. I thought it would be my secret and that I would never tell anyone. Only Lady knew what happened that day and being man's best friend, I knew she would never utter a word.

The next morning I awoke to my sister walking around the kitchen. I waited until her partner left and then said, "Karen, I need to talk with you." I told Karen about my trip, about the depression I felt over watching television constantly. Listening to reporters talk about Iraq, listening to the horrible stories about people being hung upside down on bridges and their bodies burned, listening to reporters talk about terrorism and finally the culmination of listening to the World War II Memorial dedication ceremony, resulted in my feeling so overwhelmed that I felt the need to take my own life. My sister, Karen, is a nurse and she wanted to take me to the hospital immediately. I told her I would be okay and that I felt better. I told her that I needed to take myself to the VA and check myself in for treatment. I finally admitted I needed help from the VA. This was a road trip I couldn't do alone. I had tried for more than 21 years to go it alone, but this time I knew it was different. It's not the first time I sought help nor was it the first time I contemplated suicide either. My first real thoughts of suicide happened while I was stationed in Germany. I didn't realize I had PTSD until nearly 5 years after I returned from Europe and then when I finally realized my reckless behavior was associated in some part to my experiences in Europe, I tried to hide it from anyone and everyone. Isolation is a way to hide it, so for many, many years, I became isolated, only spending time with my son and working to make a living. Yet the treatment I underwent in July 2003, in Jackson, Tennessee, to cope with my PTSD (Post Traumatic Stress Disorder) was insufficient. I knew it and the doctor knew it. My doctor had informed me that he was not trained to treat war veterans and that I would do well to contact the Department of Veterans Affairs in Memphis, Tennessee. It was time for me to acknowledge the horrible experience I went through while stationed at Rhein Main Air Base, in Frankfurt, Germany, in the early 80's, October 23, 1983, to be exact.

I drove to the Department of Veterans Affairs, located on Ninth and Colorado, in Denver. It is difficult to find parking at the VA, but that day I managed to get a spot on the very first floor. I was crying because for the first time in my life, I was admitting that I had a very serious problem and I couldn't fix it. Living was more important to me now. I wanted my haunting memories to stop. I no longer wanted to wake up thinking about those dead Marines. Neither did I want to go to bed and be thinking about them too. Everywhere I turned, everyone was talking about terrorism. It was real to everyone now, not just me. After the events of September 11, 2001, Americans understood what I had experienced and witnessed 18 years prior. Most troubling though, I left the bombings in Europe behind…but they followed me and there was no escaping now.

When I got out of my car, I didn't know where to go. Wiping my eyes and trying to find my way into the VA, I met a young couple and asked them if they knew where the emergency room was located. They both saw that I had been crying and the woman offered to walk me to the emergency room. I thanked them for their kindness and they went on to their appointment. They were obviously very familiar with the VA because they walked me through the doors, down the hallway and up the elevator to the main floor and then to the emergency room. I never would have found my way there and by the time I did, I might have turned around knowing what I was about to tell everyone.

CHAPTER 3
THE CALL TO DUTY

I enlisted in the active Air Force on October 4, 1973. My parents couldn't afford to send me to college and actually, I must admit, I had applied to several colleges with no response. Most of my classmates at Rockville High School, Vernon, Connecticut, had already received their acceptance letters. I was just too proud to wait and be turned down. After all, I had been the President of the Future Teachers Club, the President of the GAAC (Girls Athletics Activities Club), the Dean's Award winner, voted the most athletic, winning athletic awards and championships during my four years in high school. No way was I going to the mailbox to receive my "sorry you're not accepted letter." The next best thing for me was to follow in my sisters' and brother's footsteps and join the military. Not only would I get a free education, but I would see the "world" while earning my degree.

My senior year at high school was pretty difficult to say the least. It's a wonder I even graduated with all the pressure I felt from home. Fortunately, I had two people in my life who really cared about me and loved me, Linda Hyder and Grace Seeker; both of whom were my English teachers. I'll be talking more about them throughout the book. After I enlisted in the inactive reserves, that is, raising my hand and taking my oath; I received notice from the University of Connecticut Dean of Admissions that I had been accepted to the University beginning September! You have to understand me at this point. I have this "PRIDE" thing and I wasn't about to admit I made a mistake, so on October 4, 1973, I left Bradley International airport for San Antonio, Texas, to begin basic training. Mrs. Hyder and Ms. Seeker took me to the recruiter's office to see me off. Linda had given me a letter that said I wasn't to open the letter until I got onboard the aircraft. I won't share the contents of that letter with anyone, but it is sufficient to say that the words of wisdom from Mrs. Hyder actually helped me make it through basic training. I often read that letter she wrote to me throughout my Air Force career whenever I needed to gain strength to get me through.

I decided to work on writing my book again after this evening when I got on Classmates.com and read a note in the message center about another Rockville High School English teacher, Anna Bair. She was my creative writing and senior English teacher. Someone left a note saying, "Do you remember Ms. Bair?" How could anyone who had Ms. Bair for an English teacher ever forget her? I was saddened to hear she passed on but no one lives forever. I was reminded tonight that she was very disappointed when I chose to enter the military. I remember the day I went into her room to tell her I was going to join the military. Instead of encouraging me she said in a very harsh voice, "You're making a big mistake with your life. You're going to be a nobody when you can be a somebody." Those words stuck with me for my entire 19 years in the military. I wanted to prove to her that I was somebody. Looking back now, I never needed to prove anything to anyone but myself. I was never satisfied with my success, I always wanted more.

Life's lesson: Be happy and get satisfied! Life is so short and so very precious. It took me nearly a month's stay in the Denver VA hospital to realize one of life's lessons. I should have stayed for about six months really, but my finances were stacking up and I had an opportunity to take a job after being out of work for more than eight months. Can you believe it? After being out of work eight months, I finally decide to get help at the VA and I start getting phone calls for job interviews. Dr. Sturgis, one of the VA Psychiatrists, wanted me to attend a treatment center in Menlo Park, California, but as it turned out, I was making phone calls from the Psych Ward talking to perspective employers about work. I managed to secure an interview and as a result, asked Dr. Sturgis for a pass so I could attend the interview. I want you to stop now and get a mental "no pun intended" image. Imagine what I had to do in order to interview. It was definitely a sight to behold. I had leave the Denver VA, drive home to Littleton, Colorado, dress up in a business suit, and drive to the interviewing location in Englewood, Colorado. I then had to sit through the interview and then return to the hospital in time for lights out. Imagine me now coming from the interview, stepping into the elevator at the VA hospital wearing a Dana Buchman business suit, going up to the 7th floor or was it 6th? Okay...I think it was the 7th floor. Meanwhile, I looked like a well-dressed psychiatrist. As I stepped out from the elevator, the mental health patients I was attending classes with every day, didn't recognize me. I never removed my hospital band from my right arm either. During the entire interview I was waiting for someone to ask me about the white wristband. So many people are wearing colorful wristbands these days, no one even bothered to ask. The following morning after the interview, I was offered a position from Southland Corporation as a Field Consultant for 7-Eleven. Though I only worked for 7-Eleven for three months, I regretted not finishing my treatment program. Then again, anyone working for 7-Eleven should seek psychiatric help. The turnover rate was above 70 percent when I entered training. I desperately needed a job and needed to get back in the workforce. I remember Doctor Sturgis telling me, "You're only 'half baked' Bonnie, but I'll release you. I wish you the best." I had the VA social worker write in my file that I could attend a PTSD program at a later date.

By now, you're wondering why I have PTSD. First, I wonder how many of you really understand PTSD. The fastest way to find out about PTSD is to use the Google search engine and key in the word: PTSD. You'll get plenty of information. In short though, I chose to call my book, "Locked in Time" for a reason. Once you get into the tunnel it's hard to come out and once you're out, it's a scary world. It's still hard for me to talk about it or better yet, even write about it. I think I'll stop here right now. It's 9:53 p.m. on April 5, 2005, and only 18 pages written. This is going to take me longer than I thought!

It's 4:48 a.m. April 6, 2005. I slept sporadically through the night wondering when and what I would write when I awoke. As always and as it has been for the last twenty-one years of my life, I go to bed thinking about those 241 Marines who died in their sleeping bags at the Beirut Barracks in Lebanon and I wake up thinking about them. There has never been a day in my life after that tragic bombing that I failed to think about them.

I was stationed at Rhein Main Air Base in Frankfurt, Germany, but was attending a Noncommissioned Officers' School Banquet for one of my NCOs at McGuire Air Force Base. I usually flew in for the one-day event, representing the base. Of course, I just happened to rent a car and drive to Connecticut this time to see my parents. On my way back to McGuire Air Force Base, New Jersey, I had the radio playing and suddenly a news flash came across the radio. "The Marine Barracks in Beirut had been blown up and, supposedly, hundreds of military men were tragically killed." That's all I remember hearing--something about a Marine Barracks being blown up and the rest of the flight back to Frankfurt was a complete blur. I spent the next seven hours on October 23, 1983, thinking about how I was going to handle the mass casualty coming into Frankfurt. As the new Lieutenant on base, I had been assigned the additional duty as the Mass Casualty Officer for our Squadron, as well as every other additional duty. Such was the military. Give every job to the new person on base and stack them up with all types of work to give them an opportunity to "succeed." Failure was never in anyone's vocabulary. Every Lieutenant succeeded or never became a Captain. After spending nearly six years as an enlisted member I wasn't about to fail at anything. Prior Air Force enlisted members who transitioned to the officer corps hardly ever failed. Typically, those who were successful in the enlisted ranks were also successful as officers. Very few prior service officers, as we were called, ever failed.

Those who failed did so miserably. I suppose my success, as I prefer to consider it, was simply based on my understanding the people who served in the enlisted ranks. I knew what they thought about officers and I earned their respect because I once wore stripes too. After all, I remember picking up cigarette butts in the parking lots, going through dorm inspections, standing at attention on cold mornings and eating in the "Chow" hall.

The first time I walked into the Officer's club was immediately after I received my commission on January 13, 1981. I was assigned to the 436th Civil Engineering Squadron at Dover Air Force Base, Delaware, at the time. I was actually looking around to see if anyone was watching me as I approached the doors to the officers' club. I strutted like a peacock up to the doors. It's amazing what went through my mind. I uttered words something to the effect, "I've made it, I'm actually walking into the Officers' Club," a place formerly off limits to me as an enlisted member. If anyone had seen me talking to myself, I probably would have been stripped of my rank right then and there. How could I think I "made it simply because I could use the officers' club now?" The majority of the enlisted ranks considered walking into the officers' club punishment. Very few officers knew it though! No enlisted person in their right mind wanted to walk in that place, if only because we would have to salute an entire cadre of officers and as an enlisted member, we all thought officers "thought they were better than anyone else." Most of them did actually. Occasionally you would find a good officer in the ranks, an enlisted man's man, so to speak; and usually after doing research on the officer, you would find out they too, were prior enlisted. My heart was pounding as I approached the doors and then I stepped into this magnificent red-carpeted entryway. A fabulous crystal chandelier hung from the ceiling and the room was simply elegant. Fresh flowers at the entryway, large mirrors on the wall, everything was "spit-shine" perfect. I was actually standing in "The Officers' Club." I stopped to look and was in awe of the facility. I finally "made it" – no more "chow halls." Of course I paid for my meals, and at a much higher price I might add. The prices were much higher than the Airman and NCO Clubs too, but the elegant atmosphere more than made up for the higher prices. Being an officer was truly about "appearance" and of course, leadership. I probably wouldn't have had the reaction I did, but six years of ingrained behavior that officers are treated much better than enlisted people and that the enlisted people are truly the backbone of the military, contributed to that eventful walk into the red-carpeted officers' club at Dover Air Force Base.

I faintly remember eating onboard the United 747 aircraft that day. The trip across the ocean took about seven hours. I think next to giving birth to my son, Jason, that trip to Rhein Main Air Base was the longest seven hours I ever experienced. I kept thinking about what I was about to face as the Mass Casualty Officer for my unit. I had been assigned to the 435th Field Maintenance Squadron (FMS) as a Squadron Section Commander. It's a command position but I preferred to think of it as being the Squadron Commander's Administrative Officer. My responsibilities were mostly administrative, taking care of personnel matters, administrative leaves, writing APRs (Airman Performance Reports) and OERs (Officer Effectiveness Reports), ensuring that the troop morale remained high; counseled and disciplined when necessary, and even took administrative action to discharge people who failed to "meet military standards of conduct." Then, of course, there were additional duties: Security Officer, On-the-Job Training (OJT) Officer, Disaster Preparedness Officer, Awards and Decorations Officer, Mass Casualty Officer, NTSB (National Transportation Safety Board) Representative, Combined Federal Campaign (CFC) Officer, and Air Force Association (AFA) Campaign Manager and the list goes on! Usually, the Lieutenants on base were assigned the additional duty, but the 0-6's (Colonels) got all the credit and when things didn't go right, the Lieutenants took the blame. Lord help the Lieutenant if it didn't go well. Let's just say, they had a short-lived officer career...like four years. Such was life as a young Lieutenant. The Lieutenants would do all the work behind the scenes and let the "big wigs" take the credit. Now I understand why most enlisted people actually hated officers. Very few military officers ever gave credit where credit was due. The officers who did recognize people for their contribution usually had the support of the "backbone." I like to think my troops all supported me, after all, I knew what they thought, how they thought and I wasn't about to be just an "ordinary" officer. I took great pride in having worn those stripes once and it gave me an advantage over most officers. Trust me, I understood them and they understood me.

We arrived at Rhein Main and I immediately reported to the squadron. Major Samuel Swaim was my Commander and Colonel Carl Vicenzo was the Wing Commander. Major Swaim appeared to be "overly-relaxed" and "laid back" most of the time. In fact, he was too laid back for my style of leadership, but I think that's why I was assigned to the Squadron in the first place. I had strong administrative skills and I usually asserted myself in such a way that my command presence was admired. I never felt intimidated by working around male counterparts. I displayed undying loyalty to my commanders, to my people, and as a result, I was rewarded with several commendation medals and meritorious service medals throughout my Air Force career. It was rare to see a young Lieutenant with so many ribbons and such accolades. Of course, I had Colonel Richard Scrafford, the Commander of the 436th Civil Engineering Squadron at Dover Air Force Base, Delaware, to thank for much of my early success. Colonel "Dick" Scrafford was one of the finest Air Force officers I've ever had the opportunity to serve. He was a remarkable leader with such extraordinary abilities to make things happen. Let's just say, he's one of kind.

Somewhere between arriving at Rhein Main Air Base that day and meeting with Major Swaim, I knew D-Day had arrived and all the preparation and practice we did would go out the window and a new chapter would be written on how to handle the hundreds of body parts we were about to receive from Beirut. All my guys were in the barracks, and the call came about 5:30 a.m. to implement our portion of the "Mass Casualty Plan." I remember making the trip to the Field Maintenance Squadron (FMS) barracks. I walked into the rotunda and went upstairs to our unit's hall. I began knocking on the doors and informing them that we were implementing the Mass Casualty Plan and one by one I went down my list of assigned individuals. Suddenly, without having to knock on all the doors, the guys were jumping out of bed. We had about 800 people in the squadron and probably about ten percent were assigned to the additional duty. One by one, folks peeked out their bedrooms and some men and women stood in the hallway. They knew why I was there and they knew what I had come to request. Initially, before mass body bags arrived, I needed about 18 people to help. Many of us practiced but never thought we would be called to such duty. Who would imagine having to do this duty? I certainly thought there might be a possibility, but remote during my career. After all, I enlisted in the Air Force in 1973, just shortly before the Vietnam War ended.

As I watched people come out of their rooms, it was truly amazing. The rotunda reminded me of the Capitol building in Washington, D.C. actually. Not as elegant of course, but the marble structure was similar. The troops grew silent waiting for me to speak. By now, everyone had come out of his or her room. I paused a moment, and even remember swallowing before I spoke. I believe I went back down to the bottom of the rotunda. Some troops followed me down the stairs. I wanted to be certain everyone would be able to hear me. I couldn't help but remember those faces, all looking down at me. They knew what I was about to ask of them and they waited for me to speak. I took a deep breath and said something to the effect, "Many of you have practiced with me and it wasn't much practice, but now we have the real thing. I need 18 people immediately to come with me to assist in the recovery and identification of the military men who were killed in the bombing of the Marine Barracks in Beirut. We're going to remove body bags from the aircraft and assist the medical corps with the identification of these men. I don't know how many, but I know it's a whole barracks and those men were in their sleeping bags sleeping when they were blown up." I stopped to see their reaction. Some of these men and women were only 18 and 19 years old. This was their first assignment out of basic training and now, they would be called to duty to witness their comrades blown to pieces and help identify them. How could I ask this of these young people? I didn't know what I was going to face, let alone give them any idea of what they would be facing. Suddenly, a voice from the hall said, "Lieutenant, I can't do that. I just can't do it. It's going to make me sick, I can't. I'm on the list, but I can't, please don't make me go." When I fixed on who was speaking, I literally saw pain and grief in this man's eyes. He was the smart one. "Okay," I said. "Probably a lot of people feel that way, so it's best, even though we practiced that I take volunteers for this." I made a decision on the spot to accept volunteers because no one really knows how they will react in this type of situation, but I knew I couldn't back out. I was an officer and as an officer I had to remain calm and strong for my people. My only thought was to aid the medical officers in identifying those men who sacrificed so much for our country and to return them home to their loved ones with the same dignity with which they served. I said, once again, "I'll take 18 volunteers." Some of the guys began to shut the doors to their rooms, ever so quietly and slowly. Almost shutting their door in disgrace, as if they had let me down. They knew better though and they knew how they might react. I don't hold anything against them for not volunteering. Who wants to be left with such memories anyway? Then Staff Sergeant Dorffner, one of guys who was always getting into trouble stepped forward and said, "Lieutenant, count me in." Then another and another and another stepped forward until it seemed like I had more volunteers than I knew what to do with. I told the rest of the folks to report to the squadron and as we needed people, we would come get them.

Our first task was to go out on the flight line and retrieve the few body bags that had already arrived. We really had it easy, compared to the guys in Beirut. The task to identify remains is tremendous and the behind the scenes truly amazing to watch.

By now the media had gotten wind of the fact that the bodies were arriving at Rhein Main but they were unaware that we were going to do the recovery operations in the "back 9" as we called it. The Civil Engineering Squadron was erecting tents; the services folks were preparing the refrigeration trucks; the medical staff were all implementing their portion of the mass casualty plan. Everyone was getting in place and facilities were being constructed. It's what the Prime Beef Team referred to as "Bare Base Operations." They constructed a huge tent where we would place all the bodies.

While I was serving as the Squadron Section Commander for the Field Maintenance Squadron, I was also filling in as one of the Wing Executive Officers. I was in transition actually because Colonel Carl Vicenzo, the Wing Commander, had come down to my office and asked me a month prior to serve as his Wing Executive Officer. As a young Lieutenant, that's a distinct privilege actually, reserved for more senior officers. Colonel Vicenzo deserves mentioning not because he was a fine officer but rather because he was a male chauvinist pig. I must say though, it was an amazing site to see him "toss his cookies" after he smelled the wretched stench of decayed dead bodies. He never stayed in the tents too long, at least not like the rest of us.

As I said, the media got wind that we were receiving the bodies, so we devised a plan to divert the media's attention away from Rhein Main. Somewhere in the plan or some senior officer decided to make a large run downtown with refrigeration trucks to the Frankfurt morgue. I think we sent about six or seven trucks downtown and apparently the media took the bait and off they went. I never really saw the trucks leave the base, but if it worked, it was a good idea. My hat goes off to the person who suggested the diversion. The media is good in many instances, but in matters of death, especially among the military, preserving the honor and dignity of our troops is first and foremost. While in the Air Force, I once served on the military honor guard as an enlisted member. In fact, I met my ex-husband, Master Sergeant Fernando Caceres, while serving on the honor guard. He was the NCO in charge of the Honor Guard detail at Castle Air Force Base in Merced, California. The first time I met Andy, I remember tickling him under the chin with my white gloves as he was standing at attention and I was moving past him to get into my position. The guys on the Honor Guard team never let him live that one down…and during our practice sessions, the guys would tickle him under the chin with their white gloves…and some, would smack him on the cheek. At the time I did that, I didn't realize he was in charge of the team. The second time our eyes met…we were in Reno, Nevada, participating in a burial detail for a deceased military woman. Andy was standing at one end of the coffin and I was standing at the other end. We had a long-winded preacher and I remember thinking, "I'm going to pass out if he doesn't stop." My legs were getting weaker as I stood in the sand. It was so hot--it must have been at least 110 degrees. We were in full military dress; preparing to fold the America flag when Andy looked into my eyes. I knew then, at that moment, that Andy would be the one man I would love forever. On the flight back to Merced, Andy sat in the seat in front of me. As he got up to depart the plane, he asked me if I wanted to meet him at the base pool. It was his way of asking me out on a date. A year later we were married. If anyone knew about military protocol, we certainly did. I think every military member understands what military honors are about and only those serving understand the importance of preserving the dignity of our fallen heroes.

I remember recently there was a great deal of flack about the photos of the flagged draped coffins returning from Iraq. Quite frankly, I think it is most honorable to show those photos because it shows the dignity and seriousness of how our military troops render honors to their comrades. In my personal opinion, the only reason President Bush elects not to show these current photos of our returning soldiers from the Middle East is political. The American people should see the "cost of war." Now, taking photos inside a tent, with body remains up on gurneys while dentists and pathologist are poking through remains is another story. If the media had been present during that time, I'm sure they would have garnered journalist awards for such photos. Yet, had any military person caught them taking photos, I dare say they would have not only lost their film, but their camera as well.

The tents were erected and the bodies kept coming in. One by one, body bags were transported to the refrigeration trucks. I don't know how many days passed; but I know it took nearly 30 days to finally identify the last Marine and he was identified just before Thanksgiving Day. It was such a long, tedious and gruesome task. As I recall, the last soldier to be identified had only an elbow or a small part of his arm in the casket.

When I woke up this morning to begin writing on day two, I woke up thinking about Sergeant Kauffman who was assigned to the Civil Engineering Squadron. I remember he was always in the tent or around the mortuary site. If anyone needed anything, they called Sergeant Kauffman. I wondered, when I woke up this morning, how he was doing. I wondered if he was even alive. He stayed out at the site more than anyone I knew and, in fact, people began to worry about him toward the end. I think he had too much exposure but who knows how much exposure is enough? Sometimes people won't know until years later. Sergeant Kauffman must have lost it though through the years because I remember the "dead" stare in his eyes and the "iced" look he had. Many of us had to detach ourselves from what we saw. I was no exception that's for sure. Of course, I'll keep reminding you that I was an officer and as an officer, we had to be tough and strong for our troops. Even more important, I was a female officer and any female officer who was considered "mousy" or "weak", just didn't get promoted. I didn't come this far in my military career to not make rank because I was "mousy". So, Lieutenant Caceres (Tierney) "Lt. C," as I was often referred to, managed to support the troops, stay in the tents from morning until night but not nearly as long as Sergeant Kauffman. He must be one messed up fellow – if he's alive!

I've heard it said that more Vietnam Veterans committed suicide than died in the Vietnam War. PTSD really takes control of your mind if you let it…and the problem is, you can't help it sometimes.

Day after day we moved body parts from one bag to another. I remember one particular day I was helping a young airman pick up a body bag. He was standing at the top of the bag, let's just say north and I was standing south, and in between we held the remains of soldiers. The bag wasn't completely zipped and a leg fell out and off into my hands. I caught it before it hit the ground and liquid was oozing out and then I saw maggots eating the leg. My fingers went inside his leg, and it reminded me of the days on the farm when I would pick "rotten tomatoes" and my fingers would get tangled in the vines and I would pick a rotten tomato. The smell was so bad I would often wash my hands in the field with a good tomato to take away the stench. The stench was horrible. Nothing could be worse than smelling decayed bodies, not just one body, but hundreds of decayed body parts. To this day, I have a hard time swallowing as I think about what I saw during that month. I remember the smell like it was yesterday. The smell remains with you in your nostrils forever…it's unimaginable really. I faintly remember the people with whom I worked but I remember being horrified by what I saw when we uncovered all the remains of the later identified 241 Marines.

Imagine walking into a circus tent and seeing hundreds and hundreds of body bags lying on the floor. That's exactly what it reminded me of…a circus tent. Day after day the doctors worked to identify the soldiers. We transported bodies to the medical tables and transported them back to refrigeration trucks. We placed tags on those who were identified, cleaned the body parts from the sand and debris and placed their remains in stainless coffins, bright shiny coffins. One by one, they were moved to different sections in the tent. Then the doctors would find the remains of a person who was already identified and we would return those parts to the coffins. It was some sight to behold.

I can't quite remember how many days into the identification and processing of the Marines that I experienced a detachment of my body but it might have been, as best as I can remember, about a week after we started identifying the bodies. Up until then, I kept telling myself this was my duty as an officer of the United States Air Force and as a member of the military, it was my duty to return these soldiers home with the same dignity to which they served. I kept seeing body parts one after another. I'd see a head, then a face with half a head, then brains, arms, legs, fingers, and headless men. At one point early on, I remember standing in the middle of the tent and speaking to an older Senior Master Sergeant. I said something to the effect, "My God, never let it be said that black men didn't serve their country well," and the Sergeant looked at me and said very quietly, "Lieutenant, those are not black men. They are decayed bodies!" It hit me right then and there; they were decayed bodies - dead Marines who died senselessly in their sleep. The Sergeant continued as we both stood and stared across the tent, he said, "I was in Vietnam, and I never saw anything like this." I looked at him and I wanted to puke my guts up; but I couldn't do it. It's as if everything inside me wanted to come out, but I just held it in. I had to be strong for him now. As I looked again at the Sergeant, I saw tears rolling down his face and he turned from me and wiped his eyes. I'll never forget seeing him, standing there next to me, educating me as most senior NCOs educated their young Lieutenants. I couldn't imagine anything being worse than Vietnam, but then I was never there. I couldn't imagine him having to bear yet another burden in his military career. I just reached over and put my right arm around his shoulder and said, "I'm lucky to have you by my side, Sergeant. Thank you for your sacrifice to our country." He wanted to forget Vietnam I'm sure, but right in front of him was Vietnam all over again. How he made it through the day, I'll never know. I guess feeling the warmth of my hand to comfort him in his sorrow gave him strength. There were times to be tough but there were also times to say nothing – just offer a nod, a shoulder to cry on and a sympathetic ear. The greatest asset an officer has is the ability to listen.

There was a point in the identification process where it suddenly hit me again, that I was helping to identify the Marines killed in the tragic bombing of the Beirut barracks. I was standing in the tent after returning from breakfast and in the corner there was a soldier lying on the floor. He was unlike the others. He was whole. He was the first whole bodied Marine I saw. I'm literally shaking at this moment as I remember him. My hands are cold and I'm trembling and trying to keep my fingers on the keys. My stomach is sick and I have this pain deep within me at this very moment. Nothing affected me more than seeing this man in his sleeping bag. His stomach was bloated and dirt and cement pieces covered his body. He was decayed, dark, almost a dark gray. I walked closer to look at him and as I looked down upon him, I noticed his right leg looked as if someone had taken a can opener and pried his skin up. Then I noticed his jock strap had been blown off him, as he lay nearly naked in his sleeping bag. He was a tall man and heavy set, muscular like I would imagine a Marine to be. He had very little hair, like most Marines. He was someone's husband, someone's father maybe and someone's son. He was a Marine and he died so senselessly. I stepped back at the very moment I realized he was a human being. Up until now, I was putting together pieces and parts of people, but certainly, they were not human. Not until I saw "HIM." I remember stepping back and immediately saying to myself, "Is this what I'm raising my son for? Is this the life I want for my own son? My God, My God, how could you have let such an atrocity happen? These were innocent men just sleeping in their beds." That image of the young man has haunted me nearly every day of my life and as I lay here in my own bed writing this, I have tears swelling up in my eyes. The pain I feel is so deep. The pit of my stomach hurts, I just want to get sick and throw up right now but I'm holding it in. My throat hurts. Have you ever cried so much that your throat hurts? Have you ever tried to hold back tears? It hurts even worse. Okay…so I'm gaining my military composure now, taking a few breaths and remembering that I'm in Aurora, Colorado, in my bedroom, and not in the tent. My body is shaking. Maybe I should take a rest. It's 8:13 a.m. and I need to get some coffee and come back to reality. Something is pressing me to keep going. I don't want to start rambling. I want to keep your interest.

As I stepped back from "HIM" and my thoughts remained focused on my own son, I then detached from my body. I only came to know the exact time I detached after nearly 20 years of living with PTSD. The real killer, I didn't know I was living with PTSD while on active duty, until many, many years after I left the military. After all, I was not only a military officer, but I was also a mother of a five-year-old boy. It's only natural that I would wonder about the young man before me. Who was his mother and how would she react when she heard the terrible news that her son died in a tragic and senseless bombing?

At the time I detached, and I use the word detached because in order to continue with the process of helping to identify the bodies, I had to be strong and had to think what I was doing was necessary in order to honor those who died in the Marine Barracks. I, Bonnie Tierney Caceres, died that moment I saw that Marine. I left my body and became someone else that day. I physically felt my heart stop and saw my heart and soul leave my body. It wasn't until years later that I realized I entrusted my heart to two people I have loved with all of my heart. My mother, Myrtle Theresa Durkee Tierney, and Grace Seeker, my high school English teacher and the woman I would love in my heart for the rest of my life. They stood there in that tent with me and they took my heart and held it ever so gently. I knew my heart would be in safe keeping because each of them cared about me in a very special way.

CHAPTER 4

THE LOVE IN MY HEART

I met Grace Seeker in my sophomore year at Rockville High School when I had her as my English teacher. I remember the first day I walked into her classroom. I had been wandering around Rockville High (RHS) looking for her room. I was just a few minutes late as I walked into her class. I wasn't good with directions and the school was so much larger than Sykes where I attended my freshman year. As I walked into Miss Seeker's class, I remember everyone was already seated and this young "old-maid" looking teacher, with her hair tied back in a pony tail, wearing a blue and white dress and very tall high heeled shoes, pointed at me and said, "You, nim-wit, sit over there in that last row." I looked at her and said to myself, "Did she just call me nim-wit?" Then I said, "Did you call me nim-wit?" "Yes, I did" she said, "Sit down over there," while pointing to the last row and the second seat. She wasn't more than 24 years old at the time, but she sure got my attention that day. I must admit, I was a bit angry at some teacher I didn't even know calling me nim wit. How dare her I thought. It's going to be a long year for sure, I thought.

Actually, Miss Seeker and I became good friends through the years. In 1975, she was my maid of honor at my wedding. I had traveled from Castle Air Force Base, Merced, California, where I met my future husband, all the way back to Connecticut to get married. Grace was my maid of honor and I couldn't have been happier. Well, I know how I could have been happier, but that wasn't to be.
The day of my wedding, my father started smoking again. I guess the pressure of walking me down the aisle caused him to take up smoking again. I don't know how long he gave up smoking but he certainly puffed his way almost up to point of walking me down the aisle.

Grace and I became good friends in my junior year in high school. I always liked Grace, despite her calling me nim wit on the first day of class. She was a good teacher and although she played favorites, always calling on the guys and talking about football with them, she did like me. I gave her the nickname "Big Shoes" shortly after she called me nim-wit. It was my way of paying her back I guess. From what I understand, that name stuck with her throughout her 36-year teaching career. I guess it was better than calling her "swivel hips" like we called our girl's gym teacher, Gloria Limbo. Gloria used to wear this pleated skirt and whenever she walked, the skirt would shake all over the place, hence the name, swivel hips. I liked Gloria Limbo. She was my high school gym teacher and she and Pepper Trenton would always play badminton with me. It took two of them to beat me as I recall. When I worked

with the Women's Basketball Hall of Fame years later, I
sent Gloria a T-Shirt signed by all the great female players,
including Nancy Lieberman Kline, Luis Harris, Sheryl
Swoops and Annie Donnovan. She appreciated the gift
because one day out of the blue while I was living in
Medon, Tennessee, after getting out of the military, I
received a call from Gloria thanking me for the T-Shirt.

As I said earlier, I grew up on a farm or at least worked the
farm in the summer after school let out so I could earn
some money. Grace and Linda came out to the farm once to
pick tomatoes. Now that was a sight for soar eyes. Linda
came dressed in her Sunday best and Grace looked like she
was going to ride a horse. I never laughed so hard in all my
life. Watching these two ladies pick tomatoes was better
than watching the Three Stooges reruns or I Love Lucy.
They were two misfits in a tomato field having fun. I even
videotaped them walking around in the dirt. Linda was in
high heels and a skirt and Grace in her tight-fitted jeans. I
thought Grace would bust a hole in her pants but she didn't
and I was quite happy she didn't. After all, I don't think she
would have looked right in my Uncle's pants. Only I was
allowed to wear his boots and pants. At 16, I actually wore
a size eight men's shoe and my pants were 36w 29L. My
Uncle Jake and I wore the same clothes.

I remember one day coming home from the farm and I
changed my clothes in my mother's room. I don't
remember why I went into my mother's room, but I did.
Most likely, my younger sister, Robin, whom I shared a
room with was in the room sleeping or cleaning or having
friends over. Anyway, I left the clothes on my mother's bed
and in the evening when my father came home, he went
into the room and suddenly came out of the room yelling at

my mother. I was watching TV at the time and he was yelling something about "Whose pants are these and whose shoes are these? Have you had a man in the house while I was gone?" My mother was shocked and didn't know what to make of his comments and all I could do was sit in the living room and laugh. My mother flew into the bedroom and looked at the pants lying on her bed and was about as shocked as my father was. I thought, I better put an end to this or my father is going to kill my mother. I jumped up from the living room couch and said, "Hey, I wore Uncle Jake's clothes. They're his but I wore them." My mother looked relieved and my father embarrassed. He never apologized that's just the way he was, but I knew he was relieved to find out they were not some other man's clothes. Meanwhile, my mother began yelling at me for wearing men's clothes. I told her they were more comfortable than the girl's clothes and much more durable. She just accepted my answer. Of course, I loved wearing men's clothes. If I could have had my way, I would have dressed in men's clothes going to school. After all, I was a "Tom Boy," rode a motorcycle to school, played sports and beat all the guys in almost everything. I was also the first woman to take woodworking in my high school. My mother put a name to it one day, when she asked me, "Are you a lesbian?" I never heard that name before, but the way she said it, it didn't sound nice at all. In fact, it sounded down right dirty. I looked at her and said, "I am not!" She never said anything else. I suppose she knew deep down but figured she shouldn't open Pandora's box, because if I weren't a lesbian, I would certainly find out about it now. My mother knew me better than anyone else and she also knew I was curious.

The day after she called me a lesbian, I went to the school

library and looked the word up in the dictionary. When I read the definition, I looked around to see if anyone was looking at me reading. You have to understand, it was the late 60's and women were just beginning to "come out of the closet." Finally, someone had put a word on what I was feeling and at that point, I finally realized I wasn't alone in the world. There were others like me! What a relief to know that I wasn't weird after all. Of course, society has a hard time accepting gays and although nearly 36 years have passed, people still have problems with accepting homosexuality. Of course, I never acted on my homosexuality, at least not while I was married, but then again, I married to prove to myself that I wasn't. How wrong that was of me to marry a man when I knew I loved someone else and a woman at that!

Grace was in my wedding party. She was my maid of honor and on June 21, 1975, I was standing in my mother's bedroom dressed in my wedding gown and just the two of us were in there. I was thinking about a lot of things that day, but at that moment I remembered saying, "Something old, something new, something borrowed and something blue" and with that, I took the Jade ring that Grace had given me when I left for the Air Force off my "wedding finger" and pinned the ring underneath my wedding gown right next to my heart. The ring never left my finger from the day she gave it to me which was in August of 1973, just before I left for basic training. I didn't remember the incident until recently actually. Now, years later, I realized I was telling Grace without speaking, that she would always have a place in my heart forever. Since that day, she has.

CHAPTER 5

THE TWO FRENCH SOLDIERS

Grace took and held my heart at Rhein Main Air Base, held it ever so gently. While I felt as though my heart was ripped from my body, I knew it was in good hands and held for safe keeping until one day, I would ask for it back.

The Marine lay there, lifeless. I couldn't move either. I was in a state of shock. Get tough "Caceres" and move on, I said to myself. I had a job to do and I wasn't about to let anyone down.

A few days had passed and I received a call on the "brick" (Air Force two-way radio), from Colonel Vicenzo. He said he was going out to the flight line to meet a plane of DV's (distinguished visitors) and that I would be in charge of the tents. He said, "Under no circumstances, let anyone in the tent until I return." I acknowledged the call, with "Affirmative." After all, an order was an order. Since the order came from the top man on base, it was lawful, legal and moral, I wasn't about to disappoint him. That is, until two men appeared at the tent door. The sergeant on duty called me over and told me they asked to speak to the OIC (Officer in Charge). I approached the gentlemen and informed them that no one was allowed in the facility. One of the gentlemen was carrying a briefcase, dressed in an impeccable suit. He spoke with a French accent. The other gentleman was tall and lanky, almost looked as though he was from India, but I couldn't quite make out where he was from since he never spoke. The impeccably dressed man said that he was from France and that the French government suspected that we had two French soldiers mixed in with our remains and they wanted them returned immediately. "Yeah, right!" I thought. I said, "No one is allowed in this tent at all, per direction of Colonel Vicenzo." They could have cared less about the Colonel. They wanted their two soldiers and wanted them immediately. They became visibly upset when I detained them and suddenly the "official from France" pulled out a declaration paper signed by the French President ordering that the remains be returned and authorized them to search our facility for the two missing soldiers. I immediately called Colonel Vicenzo and he said once again, "Under no circumstances will you let anyone in the tent" and further explained that he had members of Congress onboard the aircraft and they were deplaning the aircraft so he had to attend to more pressing matters. He had more pressing matters than a head of state, the French President, ordering the return of two missing French soldiers. I thought to myself, "You've got to be kidding." Okay, this is where officers get paid the big bucks I thought. Time to make a decision and he did put me in charge of the tent when he left. Yet he told me not to let anyone in either. I looked at the paper once again and determined that these men could not have received access to the base without the Colonel's expressed approval and because he couldn't be in two places at once, not to mention I was holding a document signed by French President Mitterand, I decided to allow the men into the tent. The minute they came into the tent, they began ordering the removal of all the containers from the refrigeration trucks. I thought I was working with the White House staff the way they were giving orders. I met every request immediately. We had a full contingent of troops to assist so it took a few minutes to get all of the containers out in the open. We had already removed them, put them back, removed them again and put them back. They came in and out of the refrigeration trucks like popcorn popping in hot oil. When nearly 169 body bags and coffins had been placed on the open floor space, the "official French man" introduced me to his "Pathologist." He ordered the bags to be unzipped and ordered the coffins to be uncovered and then ordered me to follow them in a systematic review of the bodies. One by one the pathologist looked at the bodies and occasionally he would stop, put his hands into the remains and then move on to the next bodies. I saw more than I wanted to see by then. He came upon one body and he literally put his hands into the body and he said he was looking for specific things. I wasn't the expert; so all I did was make sure if he was going to take a body it was a "French soldier." After checking 100 or so body bags and remains, we stopped at one soldier. How he worked so fast was beyond me, but they apparently knew what they were looking for. The pathologist knelt down next to this one soldier and put his hands again, inside the

41

soldier's intestines and the next thing I know, he's ordering the removal of the soldier. I put my hand out and said, "Wait, how do you know this is your French soldier?" After all, they didn't conduct tests on him nor did they X-ray his bones or what was left of him. I could hardly say he was human, let alone French. The pathologist stood up and said, "How many American soldiers do you know who sleep with a French money bag?" Sure enough, the French soldier had a money belt strapped to his stomach, or at least at one point had a money belt strapped to him and now it was inside his remains. I ordered the Sergeant on duty to set his remains aside. We continued walking down, aisle after aisle, body remains after body remains and at one point, one soldier's tag came off his toe during the search and I leaned down to replace it. The smell from all the exposed bodies was unbelievable once again. Fortunately, we had some type of salve to wipe across our masks to prevent the stench from overwhelming us inside the tent. Still, men would faint and I would use smelling salts to revive them. My pockets were filled with them because people were passing out all over the place. After we opened about 160 plus body bags and metal coffins, we came upon another soldier's remains. This time, the Pathologist needed only to lean over and touch a piece of the remains of a skull. He ordered that the remains of #160 (for the sake) of identifying the French soldier to be removed. Again, I put my hand up and said, after looking inside, wondering how the hell anyone could tell who he was...American or French, "How do you know he's yours?" The Pathologist was brief and said, "How many Marines do you know have long hair on the back of their necks?"

Something so simple and yet it was missed in the recovery operation. "None, I responded. Take him." They got their two French soldiers and as I looked across the tent, I wondered once again, how many families would be destroyed when they heard about this tragic bombing. Then I thought, when I get home, I'm going to write my parents immediately and tell them, if the military ever tells you I'm dead and they order that the viewing be a closed coffin…listen to them. Don't look inside whatever you do, don't look inside. I just knew some family would look inside and be horrified at what they saw.

For those of you reading my book now, I once again say, if the military orders a closed coffin, listen with open ears. Remember your loved ones the way they were when you waved goodbye to them as they entered the military or returned back to base from leave. Just don't ever open the coffin to view the remains. It's so unnecessary. I died 241 times in the tent in the back of Rhein Main Air Base. I died over and over again as I saw the remains of those soldiers. I bore the pain – trust me I bore the pain.

My son, Jason, followed in my footsteps and joined the military about nine years ago. He's now serving during the Iraq war and I pray he will be spared from seeing death, seeing senseless killings, having to participate in recovery and identification operations. Yet I know he will. He is now stationed in Germany with his wife, Rebecca and is scheduled to go TDY (temporary duty) in September of this year. He hasn't said where he will be going, but my guess somewhere in Europe! He left in December and I haven't been back to Germany since 1985, when I left for England. It will be 20 years if I return in August. What a trip. Jason suggested I go back to Rhein Main. He wants to see where he lived and went to school. I don't think he knows how hard it will be for me to return. I don't know if I can return.

My heart pounds at the very thought of returning and remembering. It's time for lunch or at least a potty break. It's 10:25 a.m.

As I edit my manuscript...my son left for Iraq on Monday, April 30, 2007. I just returned from Wisconsin where he had been at Fort McCoy, training with an Army unit for his upcoming deployment. He was trained in Combat Life Saving tactics and I hope he listened well. I pray he and his fellow Civil Engineers will be safe and unharmed. I will be waiting for him to return in October. My heart is breaking because I am reliving this nightmare all over again. I don't want to be one of those parents – I just cannot bear the thought of my only son, my only child being blown to pieces from some IED. I asked Jason, in a desperate attempt to keep him from going to Iraq, if he wanted me to take him to Canada. I was serious as any mother could have been, especially knowing what I saw from the Beirut tragedy. I wanted to spare my son the same horror. We laughed about it and he knew I was serious. He just said, "Oh mom, you've got to be kidding. I hate this war too, but I signed up and now I have to go. I can't run and hide the rest of my life, you know that." I did know it, but for selfish reasons, I would have taken Jason away and you might have never read this book. I laughed twice in Wisconsin. The first time was when my sister, Karen, called to say goodbye to Jason. Jason and I were at the airport and we were picking up Candice his girlfriend. (He 's divorced from Rebecca by the way. When he was in Russia, she took off with another guy – so this is an updated version of what's transpiring now with Jason.) Anyway, we laughed about his personal situation. I'll have to keep our thoughts between us private, but it's sufficient to say, we laughed so hard that my sister thought Jason and I were drunk. The second time I laughed this weekend, was when Jason had the opportunity to talk with my brother Tom. My brother asked Jason for one request – for him to "bring him back a 'Camel Jockey's ear." My brother told my son that when he returned from Vietnam, he got two "Charlie's ears" and wanted to add to his 'ear' collection. I told you earlier in my writing that my brother most likely suffered from PTSD. My son, completely shocked at his Uncle's request, turned to his girlfriend Candice and said, "That's my mom's side of the family, they're sick." I told Jason, "Don't count me in on that, my brother Tom is who he is." Later on, I asked Jason, "Are the troops doing that – taking ears from the Iraqi's?" He said, "I've heard stories of ears and fingers being taken, yes, Mom." I guess anything happens in war…it's still sick. I trust my son will not honor my brother's request, but in a very sick way, I laughed because I needed to laugh. I cannot comprehend Jason going to war, so for now, I have to laugh. I've cried too much.

CHAPTER 6

HOMELAND INSECURITY

Forgive me for jumping around...please. I'm waking up to the worst snowstorm in Denver this year. It's about 5:28 a.m. and I can't sleep. I'm thinking about the morning briefing yesterday at the airport given by our screening manager. While I'm working for the Department of Homeland Security as an airport screener, I wouldn't call it the best paying job. Yesterday, the boss cut back on overtime and that worried me quite a bit, especially since I need the extra money. I would say this is the first time in 30 years that I've begun to live paycheck to paycheck. It was a bit embarrassing yesterday when I called my bank only to find out I had about $500 in my account. I know that sounds good to some people but when you're used to having $10,000 and $15,000 regularly in the account and you look and see it's down to $500 --- that's cause for great concern. So yes, my finances are a big concern and I woke up thinking about them.

Ironically, I was at work yesterday and one of the other agents walked up to me and said, "Is that Susan something standing in line over there? You know, the famous lady," as she pointed discreetly. I looked at the wrong woman because I said, "I don't know." As the line drew closer, another woman asked me if the woman in line was "Susan Serandon" and when I finally got a look at who they were pointing at, it was "Suzy Ormann," the financial expert. I said, "That's not Susan Serandon, it's Suzy Orman, Oprah's sidekick on finances." I must admit, as she got closer, she didn't look the same in person. She actually looked quite tired and her skin was very rough. Seems like television hides all the rough parts that's for sure. She had been waiting in the first class line for sometime and didn't look at all happy. The government cut back on overtime and even cut back on staff at the airport and passengers were not at all happy. First class passengers always complain anyway, thinking they deserve more because they paid for a higher priced seat. I'd love to tell them they paid the same ten-dollar fee as all the other passengers but this just wasn't the day to piss them off. As Ms. Orman approached the line, my eyes caught hers. I think she appreciated the fact that I recognized her and said something like "Thank you." I had to laugh inwardly because I think she was quite happy to have someone recognize her. We have lots of famous people passing through the airport all the time and I hardly recognize anyone. As she came through the walk through, I noticed she must have been traveling with her mother; at least it looked like her mother. Relieved she made it through the metal detector, I looked at Ms. Orman and said, "Sorry about the wait, ma'am. The government cut back on staff and overtime and I'm sure you understand 'financial cutbacks'." She looked at me, smiled and said, "I can't argue with that" and she began helping her mother with her bags. At least I calmed another passenger. It crossed my mind to walk Ms. Orman to the gate, talk a little about my own finances – free advice from the expert. Get a new job is what I was thinking…nothing else. Here it is, 12 years after I got out of the military and I'm making less money than I did 30 years earlier. I curse George Bush everyday and the decision I made to leave my good paying job in Tennessee for the "monster@match.com" woman --- the mistake of my life that I'm paying for everyday!

Yesterday, the boss told us to bring sleeping bags in to work just in case we have to remain at the airport with the rest of the people. If I keep on getting paid these low wages, I'll be sleeping in the bag in my car! I understand why people end up homeless. Housing costs are so high and people can't afford to live on minimum wage. I'd like to see George live on minimum wage. At least when Bill Clinton was in office people had fairly decent wages and he was creating jobs. Outsourcing is a bad word today. I'm living in a state where there are so many Hispanics too. Let's face it, many of the Hispanics take the low paying factory jobs and do the grunt work that most Americans don't even want to consider, but I'm not talking about those jobs being outsourced. I'm talking about the Human Resource Manager (HRM) positions and the administrative positions. My sister, Karen, once told me she got into nursing for that very reason.

CHAPTER 7

KEEPING GOOD COMPANY

S peaking of Bill Clinton, while I was an officer at Eaker Air Force Base in Blytheville, Arkansas, I had the opportunity to work with "Bill" on many different occasions. The first time I ever chatted with him was on the phone. I had just arrived from Bentwaters, England to Eaker Air Force Base and was assigned as Colonel Boudreaux's Executive Officer. He was the Base Commander and a tough old bird. No one wanted to work for him because he was thought to have eaten nails for breakfast – no one except someone who ate nails for lunch. Colonel Boudreaux's bark was bigger than his bite. This particular day, he said, "Get Bill on the line for me." I said, "Bill...Bill who?" He said, "Clinton." I responded with, "The Governor?" "Yes, the damn Governor," he said. I went into my office, placed a call to the Governor's office and as protocol goes, I should have placed Colonel Boudreaux on the line waiting for the Governor, but before I knew it, Governor Clinton was on the line. "Bill here," he said, as I seemed stunned. I said, "Governor Clinton." "Yes," he said. Still stunned I made a big protocol mistake, I said, "Colonel Boudreaux would like to speak with you, sir." "How the hell is Ray doing," he said. I said, "Fine Sir" and he said, "Don't call me Sir, just call me Bill." "Yes, sir, Governor." He said, "Who is this?" I said, "Captain Bonnie Caceres, sir." He said, "I said, don't call me sir, just call me Bill. You must be new to the base." "I am Governor," I replied, and he quickly responded by saying, "Listen, Bonnie, we're home folks down here and everyone calls me Bill, especially my friends. Now go ahead and put Ray on the phone." "Yes, sir...Bill." He was something else!

I patched the Governor through to Colonel Boudreaux and I heard Colonel "B" yell, "How the hell are you Bill? What are you doing for your country today?" Then I heard Colonel Boudreaux laugh and I stopped paying attention. I absolutely loved working with Governor Clinton whenever he came to the base. The first time I ever ate catfish was when Governor Clinton came to our open house at the base. We actually fried fish together. I'm telling you, I ate some of the best catfish in the world that day. One of the members who owned a radio station, Harold Sudbury, saw to it that I was interviewed on the radio after I ate my first catfish. I had no clue what catfish tasted like because up North, we ate Trout. I never liked Trout and in fact, choked on a fishbone once when I was a kid and never ate fish again. I think the only reason I ate fish this time was simply because I fried it with the Governor. I met the Governor at various base functions throughout my time at Eaker. I do remember; however, this one particular time standing in the street during the Blytheville Appreciation Day, a version of their city street fair. Bill was shaking hands with folks, enjoying the day and I walked up to him and said, "I need a favor." "What's that?" he remarked. Colonel Pete Giroux is leaving the base and I would like to see that he receives something special from your office for the work he's done as Base Commander. The Governor told me to contact his secretary and get some "Cotton Award" certificate. I can't quite remember, but I wrote the number down and later contacted his secretary as he said. Meanwhile, while I was looking at Bill, I had been standing on his right side and I'll be damned if he didn't look like President Kennedy. At that very moment, I said, "Damn, did anyone ever tell you, you look like President Kennedy?" He just smiled and looked at me. I said, "Okay, this is a photo op, Sir. I want my picture standing next to the 'next President.'" He hadn't announced running yet and I even asked, "Are you going to run for President? You should you know?" He said, "I wasn't thinking about it." I think I said this to him in 1990 or so. I had my picture taken with Bill and I was wearing the hottest black leather outfit and tank top. I had lost a lot of weight and looked my best ever! He put his arm around me and my friend took the photo. Years later, I was looking for that photo and it's nowhere to be found. I think my ex-partner was jealous of that photo because I never saw it after I showed it to her. I was proud of that photo but maybe she thought I was just another "Clinton" girl! Lord, he never made any pass at me at all during the time I knew him and I think I was damn good looking then. Who knows, he might have thought about it and knowing my own affinity toward woman, being with him was the furthest thing from my mind.

Now Hillary, that was another thing. She liked women in uniform I had been told. In fact, during special base visits where I had been the protocol officer in charge of making arrangements for distinguished visitors (DVs), I would often notice her looking at me. She would smile and I, of course, would smile back. I don't know if she admired me or was attracted to me. One time I was invited to some function at EB Gee's house, a prominent member in the Blytheville community. She was hosting a reception for Congressman Alexander's fiancée and Hillary was going to be in attendance. Amazingly, I received an invite to this special function. I wondered why I was being invited to this and the commander's wives were not. My hairdresser and a woman I will always consider my best friend (who's name I'll keep private), jokingly said, "I think you were invited because Hillary likes you...I mean really likes you!" "What," I said? No??? You're kidding if you think I'm going to sleep with the Governor's wife! (Not that the thought didn't cross my mind though!) I always admired Hillary very much and thought her to be a strong and confident woman. I love women who are assertive and put men in their place and she certainly kept the boys in shape. Another friend of Hillary's was Mary Gay Shipley. She owns "That Bookstore" in Blytheville and when Hillary had her first book signing after writing "It Takes a Village," Mary Gay promoted her book and had a special guest invite. I happen to have been on the list and I was very happy to attend. As it turned out, I took my friend up on stage with me to get the book signed and while Hillary had bodyguards all around, I remember Kay and I going up together. I saluted Hillary and she gave me a kiss on the cheek. There I was, standing with Kay on my right, Hillary in front of me and feeling the warmth of those lips on my cheek.

I would love to see Hillary as our First woman President...anyway...Bill would make a wonderful First Gentleman and he certainly would keep members of Congress worried about hosting "tea parties" at the White House with their wives. I love it! The American people would love it too. Better yet, I'd love to see a "Clinton-Clinton" ticket! Now that would be true "history in the making!" Well, fortunately we'll have no more "Bush" in the White House come 2008.

My good buddy Mark Warner, Governor of Virginia, should make a run for it. He's one heck of a good man. We graduated Rockville High School together back in Connecticut in 1973. Mark came from a fairly poor family like most of us. He lost the senate race the year he ran against John Warner. It was Warner vs. Warner at our 25th Rockville High School reunion. Imagine punching tickets on that race. When I knew Mark he was a staunch Nixonite. It was the first year 18 year olds could exercise their right to vote...and vote we did. I voted for Nixon too, but ever since then, I voted Democrat. I never followed Mark's career after he left for college because I enlisted in the Air Force. I just remember years later when our 25th reunion arrived, I sent a note to the reunion committee that if anyone needed help in returning or flying into the reunion that I would help. I received a note back saying that Mark Warner had that covered. Little did I know he was one of the ten richest men in Virginia, spending nearly 8M of his own money to run for the senate position in Virginia. When I made the offer to help defer transportation costs, I was just acting out of the goodness of my heart, not because I was wealthy. Mark had the money to back his offer. Hell yes, let him pay! He's a good man that's all I have to say and the American people would be fortunate to have him in the White House. I don't know if he would like to play second fiddle to Hillary but I do know he cares about the "middle man/woman" and he's just the type of person we need representing the American people. We've got Barak Obma running for President as well. I'll never forget his speech at the last Democratic National Convention. I know I said to myself, "Now that is a 'Future President'." I once wrote in the blog site on "Forward Together" that Mark Warner and Barak Obma would make a great team too. Who knows…it just might be the other way around? In any case, Mark Warner knows what a loaf of bread costs that's for sure. We had our 30th high school reunion in 2004 and Mark hosted us at the Governor's Executive Mansion in Richmond, Virginia. He hasn't changed in 30 years. He always wanted to be in politics. I videotaped him once standing in our class saying he was going to be the President of the United States one day. If God has it in his plans to make Mark Warner a future President of the United States, he surely will. God willing…he does.

So we transition from one of the richest men in Virginia to one of the poorest women in Colorado. It's 7:07 a.m. April 10, 2005, and I'm listening to the wind howl against my bedroom window. For a moment, I forgot about my finances, got lost in my military memories, and even fantasized a bit. You know, for a poor woman, I sure have kept some good company. Maybe I'm not so "POOR" after all!

Another Life Lesson: "You're really "Rich" when you surround yourself with "Good Caring People." I wonder if I can get a few hours sleep before going into work. I wonder if the airport is even open. I'll worry about that later.

CHAPTER 8
TEARS KEEP COMING

A few months have passed since I wrote the last entry and it is now July 15, a week after the London Bombing. My goodness, I worked myself to death the last few months and all this overtime has gone toward paying my bills. The end of May I gave my roommate a few months notice that I would be moving out on September 1, but ever since that time I've had a difficult time paying bills so I decided to move in with my sister again, so I'm moving out July 31. I can't seem to make ends meet on this salary so now my roommate is really upset because she's going to lose out on 475 a month. It's amazing how people can become so nasty over just a little bit of money. People can befriend you and treat you just wonderful and when things don't go right, they can easily turn into monsters. Well, I don't feel too badlybecause I did give her 30 days notice and to be honest, I stayed a few months more than I expected. She earned nine months rent and I think she's darn lucky. She wasn't the greatest person to room with anyway so I don't feel badly about leaving. I did mention the London bombing didn't I? The day after the bombing I had an appointment with my VA counselor in Denver. As I wrote previously, I try not to watch the news at all because the news just isn't good for someone with PTSD. My friend, Karen, called to ask me if I was watching the news. It was about 8:00 a.m. in the morning – maybe 9:00 a.m. Something about that 9:00 a.m. I told Karen that I didn't have the news on and she said, "Well, maybe you shouldn't watch the news today." I asked her "Why not?" She said, "Well, there's been another bombing and this time it is in London. Maybe you should stay away from the television." I asked her if anyone had been killed and she said, "Yes, about 40 people or so." My heart started to pound and then I said, "Well, I'm not going to watch it." The problem with people with PTSD, they will tell you something and do just the opposite though. Don't trust them one bit because I was so intent on watching television that I immediately turned the television on and began watching ABC news. Sure enough, every channel was covering the bombing and I began flipping channels to get as much information as I could. Apparently there were three bombings in different locations throughout London. In fact, I was very familiar with the locations because in 1985 through 1987, I was stationed at RAF Bentwaters in the United Kingdom. My son, Jason, and I would travel to London nearly every weekend and take in a few plays, enjoy a dinner and then visit Harrods. It was a ritual nearly every weekend that we would take the mass transit to London, and then ride the tube and even the double decker buses. The subway system in London was so easy to use and nearly everyone traveled on them.

I can't tell you how distressed I became because just a few days prior I had been telling folks that something terrible was going to happen. Of course, I'm always feeling like something horrible is going to happen and with my son living abroad, I am always thinking something bad is going to happen. My worst nightmare is that my son will experience the same trauma I experienced and his life will be changed forever. It's inevitable that military people will experience trauma in some fashion, especially those living abroad. Worrying about bombs in the 80's became second nature to me while I was stationed in Europe. I never thought that I would ever experience the same feelings in our own homeland. After watching the news and feeling anxious again, I decided to pop a few of my Ativan, anti-anxiety medication that I take for stressful situations. I shut the television off because the news was beginning to get to me and I resigned myself to get ready for work and avoid television all day. My mind began to wander though as I was getting ready for work. I started thinking about all those people in London who were killed and all of their families. Then the bodies of the Marine soldiers flashed in front of me once again. I saw dead Marines everywhere. I remembered myself picking up pieces and body parts and the feet and hands falling off in my own hands. I began smelling the stench of the bodies and could feel my stomach begin to tighten. A few minutes later, I felt nauseous. When will this feeling ever go away? Why do I internalize it so? When I got to work I went to Seattle's Best at the Denver airport, just outside North Checkpoint. I stopped to get my usual cup of coffee and about the time I walked into the café, I looked up at the television, with a crowd around the counter, everyone's eyes pinned to the television, I heard a reporter say, "And body parts were just strewn all over." That's all I had to hear and I immediately stepped out of line and became visibly shaken. All the medicine in the world wasn't about to keep my mind off of those comments. Body parts...just hearing those words takes me back to 1983. Almost in tears, I walked to the international terminal where we hold our 12:30 p.m. screener's meeting. I sat down in one of the chairs and it was about 11:30 a.m. I arrived at the airport early thinking that we might have extra security procedures in place as a result of the bombing and I just left the house so I wouldn't be tempted to watch any more news coverage. For security reasons, I can't divulge any information that is provided during our afternoon briefings but, nonetheless, we discussed the bombing briefly. Last month, I remember feeling quite anxious that Memorial Day was approaching and I had a difficult time at the checkpoint. In fact, about two weeks prior to Memorial Day, I had tried to contact the VA Mental Health folks and receive counseling but no one returned my call. So on May 30 when I reported to work, I had to leave the meeting in tears. I remember trying to hide my eyes. I wore glasses and tried everything to keep the tears from streaming down my face but I couldn't hold back my emotions. You see, last year during Memorial Day I ended up in the VA hospital on the psychiatric ward after thinking about killing myself. Memorial Day is just a trigger point for me and I have learned to be cognizant of that day and try to cope. As it turned out, I made an appointment after causing a big stink with the VA about the Mental Health folks not returning my call and that I didn't have a support system that was available to me when I needed it most. As a prior officer, I just can't find it in myself to shed tears in front of people and holding back tears is even more painful. What did I fear most? You know, I have to live every day of my life trying to "forget" what happened and Memorial Day is a time to remember the dead. Well, it's hard for me because I don't want to remember the dead. In fact, I have to remember 241 dead Marines and it's so difficult for me to remember them. I honored those men, but to mourn them is so painful. Needless to say, I ran up to my supervisor in complete tears and asked that I be excused. I had anticipated that the screening manager might make a few comments about Memorial Day and maybe even ask us to have a moment of silence. Do you know what it's like to ask a former military member or even a military member to have a moment of silence for dead people? It's not easy to say the least. It's too painful and it hurts like hell. It's good to cry and it's okay to cry – it took me 20 years to come to grips with crying but still, I feel embarrassed to cry and have people visibly see the pain on my face. So here I was, again in a meeting and now I was fighting back tears again. My teammates could see I was visibly upset and most of them knew I was involved in the recovery, identification and processing of the Marines killed during the terrorist bombing. Only those close friends knew the pain I was experiencing. This time I remained for the meeting. The day just seemed to linger on though. At one point during the day, I lost my breath. I began turning all shades of red. This never happened before. I actually felt as though I was choking and when one of my teammates saw me gasping for breath, he thought I was choking on something. Fearful that he was going to do the Heimlich maneuver, I managed to get my breath back. I knew if he tried the Heimlich maneuver nothing would come up and he would probably really choke the breath out of me. I almost laughed inwardly a bit because he actually scared me into breathing. I remembered a time when I was a child and my father had the hiccups all day. My mother decided that she needed to do something serious to get him to stop, so she put a bag over my father's head. While the bag was over my father's head, my mother went to the knife draw and pulled out the biggest knife she could find. I remember thinking my mother must have really been crazy and wondered what the heck she was doing with that long knife. When she lifted the bag from my father's head, she had this huge knife in her other hand and I think she must have scared the living daylights out of my father because he stopped the hiccups. Whatever she did worked and I think the fact that my father became frightened help cure him. There was no doubt I had a panic attack. Thanks to Neil, I started breathing again. I knew I needed to tell someone what happened so I walked up to my supervisor and informed her that I had a panic attack and that I was remembering the Marines in Beirut. She had a bit of a blank stare and I found myself explaining my involvement with the terrorist bombing in 1983. Most people can't even fathom what it is like to put body parts in body bags and go through what I went through. It was suffice to say, she was sympathetic and told me to do whatever I felt most comfortable doing. She was a wise woman to say that because little did she know how much I appreciated her compassion. I knew one thing for certain – I did not want to be alone and I did not want to go home. I felt secure in the airport and I felt safe. People with PTSD have difficulty feeling safe and whenever a person's security or safety is threatened, it can be dangerous. I've been told more than once that more Vietnam Vets have committed suicide than died in the Vietnam War. Astounding figures but it's true according to the Vietnam Veterans organization. I don't doubt it because I know how many times I thought about suicide myself – just to rid myself of these memories. In any case, I remained on the checkpoint that day and I'm alive today to continue writing my story.

CHAPTER 9
MY PAPER TO CONGRESS

I've seen my VA counselor twice now and I have arranged to see her every two weeks or so. The day after the London bombing, on June 8, I had my scheduled appointment. Beverly Nussbaumer, my Mental Health Nurse Practitioner, could see I was visibly upset. She opened the meeting with first asking me if I wanted to go into sexual counseling with other military women. I thought she was nuts for asking me that question. How could she ask me about sexual grief counseling when the primary reason I was seeing her dealt with my experiences with the terrorist bombing in the 80's. I'm still bothered by her sexual trauma questions. It's no wonder why VA people kill themselves – it's hard to find anyone who really understands the plight of war veterans. I remember telling her that the London bombing had taken me back again. I had a few flashbacks and she said, "Well, I just wanted to offer you counseling for the sexual trauma you experienced while in the military and with your family." I thought for sure I should have been counseling her after that comment. I responded sharply with, "I resolved my issues with family sexual abuse and with the military incidents, I'm here to deal with the trauma I experienced as a result of my involvement with the 241 Marines killed in Beirut." She said, "Well, I knew you might be feeling anxious over what happened." Anxious...was she nuts? You've got to be kidding me. Anxious was an understatement. I informed Ms. Beverly that I had this pain in the pit of my stomach, that I became visibly upset at work, lost my breath after having a panic attack and that I was still upset. I told her I popped a few "chill pills" as I prefer to call them and even they didn't relax me. I also informed her that in order to take control of the situation to the best of my ability, I had to talk to myself and tell myself that I was not in the mortuary tents, but rather I was in the airport and it wasn't 1983, but rather 2005 and I was again, at the Denver airport. My mind wanted to take me back, but I wouldn't allow it to take me this time. I was so proud of the way I handled myself and Ms. Beverly said that I did a great job. I liked hearing the reinforcement this time and I was truly proud. It's hard to pat oneself on the back...but when it comes to PTSD, every little step toward controlling bad memories is a step toward recovery. I shouldn't really use the word recovery, because no one really recovers from PTSD. People learn to live with PTSD and recognize their trigger points. Knowing those trigger points is really key to managing PTSD. This disease can kill you if you allow it too – the secret is being aware and even more important, seeking treatment and early intervention. At this point, I should say; however, Ms. Beverly Nussbaumer has been instrumental in keeping me alive and I thank her every minute that I spend time with her in the office. She is a brilliant and very caring woman. She herself served in the military and truly should be commended for her own sacrifice that she has made. I think the major reason I am donating all royalties to the Department of Veterans Affairs in Denver, Colorado, is in large part because of the help I've received from both Beverly and Charmayne – my mental health team. I can't thank them enough!

I'll have another meeting with my counselor on July 28 and I'm feeling somewhat better about what's happened. It might have to do with the fact that I took a few days' vacation to calm my nerves. Of course, my feathers got ruffled yesterday after the Department of Homeland Security Secretary, Michael Chertoff, met with Committee members on Homeland Security. I watched CSPAN and the representatives on the committee certainly did not cut him any slack. After the hearing, I drafted a three page talking paper to the members on the committee stating my position about terrorism and the way those members handled the hearing. I'll include the information I wrote in my book. In fact, I should be getting on line to see if the Committee Chairman responded to my email. I never disclosed that I myself worked for the Department of Homeland Security, but I'm almost certain some legislative staff weenie will perform a quick background check on me and find out that I actually work for the Transportation Security Administration. Who knows, I may finish my book sooner because I get fired for my comments. Here's what I sent to the hill.

PROPOSED RESTRUCTURING OF DEPT OF HOMELAND SECURITY
HEARING ON CAPITOL HILL 7/14/2005

TALKING PAPER TO COMMITTEE MEMBERS

SUBMITTED BY:

BONNIE J. TIERNEY
ADDRESS
LITTLETON, CO 80128

OVERVIEW:

I watched the CSPAN coverage of today's hearing with the recently appointed Department of Homeland Secretary, Mr. Chertoff, and the Homeland Security Committee members and I certainly understand why it's difficult to have any stability within the newly organized Department. You folks sit up there in your big leather chairs, and throw out questions after questions, some of you without allowing the Secretary to answer accordingly. You want timely reports and you want immediate action plans for mass transit, more recently concerned because of the London bombings. Do you have any idea the scope and responsibility of Mr. Chertoff's position? He and every prior/future DHS Secretary will be a scapegoat in the event of another terrorist bombing or worse yet, biological or chemical disaster. What it all amounts too is that there is nothing you nor your committee can do to stop terrorism in the United States because you have primarily focused on aviation security and the war in Iraq since September 11, 2001. Have you not forgotten that Osama Bin Laden informed both President Bush and Senator Kerry during the past elections that they had no control over terrorism?

ASSESSMENT:

Rep. Mackey, D-Mass was correct in his assessment, although his delivery and questions to the DHS Secretary were a bit ruthless...but then, so is terrorism and how it affects each of us. My concerns about terrorism stems from my own personal involvement in the very first terrorist activity perpetrated against Americans 22 years ago with the bombing of the Marine Barracks in Beirut, Lebanon, on

October 23, 1983. America was asleep then because 241 Marines died senselessly in their sleep while a suicide truck bomber stormed the gates and it wasn't until after September 11, 2001 (18 years later) that our country saw fit to find the person responsible for that bombing. I must add, those members from Congress under the Reagan/Bush Administration who traveled to Europe to view the recovery, identification and processing of the 241 Marines literally blown to pieces, managed to walk through the mortuary "tents" staying less than 3 minutes and then getting into their "Mercedes" one by one, being driven by airmen and some taking Rhein River cruises on taxpayer dollars. I know this personally because I was the Executive Officer to the Commander during their visit and one of the officers in charge of the identification and processing of those killed. Need I say I lost respect for many members of congress who traveled on taxpayer dollars on what I refer to as a "boon-doggle trip." Now, you're asking our DHS Secretary to make our homeland secure overnight! Our terrorists are getting more sophisticated and are growing up in our neighborhoods around our country. They are being "born" in our country to kill us because they find our way of life a threat to their own society and religious values. They are gaining the trust of American people and when we least expect it, they will attack us. Why is this? Americans are too trusting and our government is reactive instead of being pro-active. We all want a quick fix and we want immediate results now but folks, it's not going to happen. We, all Americans, need to think like the terrorists, anticipate their next moves, and Reps. Mackey, D.-Mass and Shays, R-Connecticut are correct in being concerned about cargo on aircraft, about biological, chemical and Al Queda threats. We are vulnerable as Americans and the public is naïve.

ACTION/RECOMMENDATION:

If passenger planes carry 22% cargo and they go unchecked, how safe is that to the American public? The public has a right to know which cargo has been checked if any – I agree. 100% check of cargo on Cruise Ships is a must!

Hazmat being transported should be "GPS" tracked and route plans submitted by truckers, similar to the aviation industry where pilots are required to file flight plans. 76% of all distribution trucks go up and down I-40.

Educate the Public and Use Them in a "Terrorist Neighborhood Watch" Program on every street in America. If someone participates in the program, give that individual a "tax advantage" for helping prevent violence in America. The city Emergency Management position can manage this program. I'm not referring to people becoming vigilantes, but rather have the public know who's your "neighbor?" Realize that some of these people who participated in the program might just be terrorists themselves. Isn't that what we worried about in Iraq with training Iraqi Security Guards? What better way to ferret out terrorists?

Establish "Business Terrorism/Security Experts" – in every private sector. Have them address their vulnerabilities in their plants, manufacturing facilities, stores, retail outlets, workforce development buildings, recreational facilities, baseball fields, convention centers, hotels, etc., and forward reports to the DHS Intelligence branch. For every business that creates a Primary Security Position at a given facility – give them a "tax break."

Rep. Mark Souder, R- Indiana suggested that DHS and all their manpower, whether TSA, Border patrol or others, assist with Drug Enforcement. He's absolutely correct. Stop drugs and you stop violence, stop drugs and you control funds for the purchase of illegal guns, chemicals, and possibly biological monies to fund bio-terrorism. While "homeland" security is the primary function for DHS, why not use manpower across the board – it's government dollars and the government should be thinking about utilizing employees in multi-faceted roles. The government needs to be structured like "private industry" at times. We had this problem with the CIA/Intelligence/FBI and lack of information and cross-flow. We need to improve our methods, technology and use people accordingly. There is no need to duplicate efforts and if it's not "Value added – get rid of it."

Want to wake a sleeping giant in America? Attack childcare centers. Did we forget the lessons of Russia recently? How many childcare centers are protected? In what ways are they protected? What systems are in place to protect our children in schools? I'm not referring to the secondary school systems either? Our future leaders are in those "elementary schools" and "childcare centers." My son followed in my footsteps and is serving in the Air Force overseas, but he spent 1/3 of his life in a childcare center. In the early 80's, I remember terrorists threatening to bomb our school buses. As a result, parents rode the buses in Germany. Americans didn't have to live with that threat, but our military men and women overseas found it to be a daily occurrence.

Rep. Nita Lowey, D. - New York was concerned about outdated identification badges used by airport employees to gain access into the airports by maintenance personnel, airline industry personnel, etc. "Everyone should walk through metal detectors, no doubt about it." However, metal detectors won't detect "explosives" unless you use "state of the art technology" explosive trace portals. They may be expensive, but then who can put a price on one person? She also suggested increased use of security and bomb dogs and I especially agree. It's getting to the point where citizens will be purchasing their own "detection devices" on mass transit to "save their own lives" in the event of a potential bombing. Unfortunately, the average middle class person will not be able to afford such devices. 250 Billion dollars has been allocated for Iraq – how much are we spending for our "homeland?" Short of purchasing "chemical masks" and "chemical suits" the public is too vulnerable. I'm sure Rep Mark Souder would agree that Bomb dogs could also serve as "drug" dogs. This would certainly cut down on potential violence in our country and possibly save many lives.

CHOKE POINTS:

Water and food supply systems must be carefully secured. It is my belief that while people are looking to the big cities for the next terrorist act, we will actually see small towns affected. Osama Bin Laden threatened to kill over 4M people on videotape released. If they attack one nuclear facility, as an example, Oak Ridge, Tennessee, they can easily achieve their goal, depending upon weather conditions and fallout. If they planned another attack at the same time they planned the September 11, 2001, attacks, it could affect every state in the United States because it only takes one person per state to cause a significant traumatic event. The lessons of September 11, 2001, should remind each of us about their capability and determination. If I wanted to attack "Russians" I would grow up in their society, live among them, befriend them and learn their ways – then I would attack when they least expected it. A forum we have seen them use to disseminate information has been in religious buildings. We have laws in our country that prohibits using the pulpit to disseminate violence, but then again, remember the days of the KKK in the South. Hate crimes and terrorism knows no laws and has no boundaries. We witnessed the results of the Oklahoma bombing. I have believed this philosophy since participating in the recovery, identification and processing of the 241 Marines killed in Beirut and yes, I have not forgotten and I will never forget. We have taken the fight abroad, but the enemy lives at "home" in each of our neighborhoods.

We have a false sense of security in our country and we "think" we are secure, or more secure than we were. In reality, we are as vulnerable as all other nations and we have "yet to see" total destruction. We must find Osama Bin Laden and derail his future plans...he is the reason September 11, 2001, happened in the first place. Let us not forget whom we are trying to find! Will it take 18 years to find him while undergoing another disaster?

CHAPTER 10
ON MY POLITICAL SOAPBOX

N ow you may have a better understanding how anything that affects terrorism affects me. I cannot sit by without feeling some type of rage over the way our government expects a quick fix to this problem. Terrorism is not going away anytime soon and the sooner Americans get their heads out of the sand, the sooner they will realize we need to take action in a big way in our country. I do believe; however, that most of our future terrorists who strike the United States will have grown up in our society and gained the trust of their American neighbors. Call me an idealist; but the truth is we have to become more serious about knowing our neighbors. We don't need to live in fear everyday but we certainly don't need to bury our heads in the sand or turn the other way either. In my opinion, for what it's worth, the next terrorist events will involve chemical or biological acts of terrorism or a strike against our water and food supply. There will be a day when Americans will wake up and listen to the news coverage that not 5,000 men, women, and children have died, but rather five million. The world as we know it will change forever and the events of that catastrophic event may very well be the advent of a nuclear war. Doomsday you say…well, if we don't act accordingly now to control weapons of mass destruction and the building of nuclear weapons worldwide, we will witness destruction in our lifetime like the world has never seen before. World War II and the killing of six million Jews were catastrophic, but those tragedies happened in Europe, not on American soil. This time; Americans will feel the pain at home, again, on our soil. History has a way of repeating itself –let's just hope and pray that we can change the course of history.

Each time I log off the computer and log on, months seem to pass. In fact, tomorrow is September 11, 2005, and we will be remembering our fallen Americans at the World Trade Center, the Pentagon and in Philadelphia at the Denver airport. Tomorrow, we take time to have a moment of silence. It seems that each time I log on to the computer something terrible happens.

Last week, Hurricane Katrina pounded New Orleans on August 29, 2005. It's now said that this is the most tragic natural disaster that has happened on American soil. What's tragic about it? Our government wasn't prepared to handle this natural disaster. New Orleans flooded from an F4 hurricane and our government failed to respond to the people in New Orleans. Certainly people knew New Orleans was in a fish bowl. Certainly there was a contingency plan for such a disaster. I'm completely overtaken by the events and thank God I have been on my medication regularly because, quite frankly, I think I might have jumped off Pikes Peak literally!

It boggles my mind that our government was so slow to respond. Of course, just as Congress called for congressional hearings, this has become one of the most divisive events in our history because we have yet to determine the number of lives lost as a result of Katrina. All I know is that Mike Brown, head of FEMA, has been dismissed from his position today, or at least in political terms, called to return to Washington. It's a nice way of letting him down easy – that is, the next thing we will hear is the President accepting Mike Brown's resignation. For those of you who are familiar with disaster preparedness and emergency planning, you will agree that all levels of government were responsible for their lack of planning and inability to have a solid evacuation plan. I've been watching CNN news coverage day after day and for the last two days, I was off from work, I watched the news non-stop until I became so depressed I couldn't get off the couch. I went to bed with an awful headache. Earlier in the week I contacted Senator Salazar's office, our Senator from Colorado, to ask him what he was doing about this disaster? The conversation went something like this:

"May I speak to Senator Salazar? This is Bonnie Tierney, a resident of Colorado." The lady on the other line said, "He's not available, may I help you?" I said, "I wish to speak to one of his staffers please." A few minutes later, a woman answered the phone. I couldn't quite make out her name but I began to tell her that I was a Major in the inactive reserves and that I was calling about the government's slow response to help the evacuees in New Orleans. I immediately asked her to elevate the information I was about to disclose to her to Senator Salazar. She said, "How can I help you?" At that point, I basically lost it. The hurricane struck Sunday and on Monday the levees began to break...or was it Tuesday. The CNN coverage showed people in water up to their waists and I made that call on my way to work from my cell phone. I said, "I'm not going to belabor the fact or question why the government didn't evacuate the residents out of the city by military airlift. "After all," I said, "I know for a fact that military aircraft are ferried out of the city during an evacuation at least 72 hours prior to bad weather." I informed the Congressman's staffer that the least the local and state government could have done was to call in military aircraft or contract with civilian airlines. There could have been at least 800 takeoffs daily during an emergency evacuation. I further informed her, "What's even worse, the news media has indicated all the people are to be taken to the Superdome in New Orleans. What I want Senator Salazar to know is that in the early 90's the military closed over 100 bases around the country. Why are you not housing those people on military bases?" Congressman Salazar's staffer responded, "That's a great idea, I'll pass that along." "Great idea," I screamed into my cell phone. "Are you kidding? You politicians must have your heads up your ass. Who the hell's in charge? People are going to die in the 1,000's and you're telling me that's a great idea. Who's planning this evacuation?" I was trying to calm my nerves because I wondered how the hell these people got jobs when they had no common sense. "Well," I told the Congressman's staffer, "They can secure cruise ships arriving from the Caribbean. Confiscate Carnival Cruise Lines' ships; Royal Caribbean, Norwegian cruise lines, Princess cruise lines.

The larger ships have the capacity to house at least 2,000-3,000 passengers on board." I wasn't very cordial and let's just say, I probably sounded like a lunatic, but then again, I didn't care. I began swearing obscenities in the phone and by then, I realized I lost the person's full attention. I couldn't help myself to be perfectly honest. I feared I might have a stroke or possibly an accident while I was driving. The veins in my neck protruded from the sides as I screamed into my cell phone. How can some of our people in government be so out of touch?

In the short time the Department of Homeland Security was established after the September 11, 2001, bombings, I cannot believe that our country was not prepared to handle a natural disaster. Surely government officials knew that New Orleans was in a bowl and at least six feet below sea level. News events, one after another, showed the terrible photos of people living in horrible conditions, wading through sewage and dead bodies floating all over. Children were crying, parents angry with the government and rightly so. Our government failed to give people food and water for over seven days. How can we, the richest country in the world have come to this? I tell you, I was so outraged because all I saw on television was poor black people and I knew this was only the beginning of what was going to soon be the big "blame game" in Washington. I'm so disgusted with our politicians that even before this disaster, I sent an email around to all my friends asking them to vote everyone out of office.

I think Americans should take back Congress. Regardless of your political affiliation, I have advocated that the American people should vote every member of Congress out of office. We need to send a message to our lawmakers letting them know that we're fed up with their politics and their independent commissions and their lack of response. American taxpaying citizens were relegated to being called "refugees" by the media – they were displaced Americans and yet the poorest of the poor were left to rot in the streets of New Orleans, many without transportation, many without assistance. Who looked after the old, the weak, the suffering, those in hospitals, and those in nursing homes?

I once said America was sleeping when the first terrorist attack was against the Marines in Beirut and I still say, "They are sleeping." It took over a week for our government to get things together and even then, it wasn't enough to stop hundreds from dying. I tell you, it's no wonder why so many Americans want to leave the country. Has America seen the tragedy really? An entire city was submerged under water and all we could do is standby and feel helpless to watch the elderly, weak and poor people drown. I'm still sick to my stomach thinking about this past week and while I'm on the bus riding home tonight, I can't wait to get to the next bit of news about the events of today.

Why do Americans vote for people without military experience? Yes, I may have known some pretty incompetent officers, but not many in my lifetime. I was blessed to work alongside of some great leaders. When you vote my friends, remember, the person you vote for as your Mayor or Governor has your lives in their hands and makes decisions that could very well affect your life. It's beyond my comprehension, why people would want an entertainer in office. This is not a statement to impugn any entertainer, but rather to make people absolutely aware of the consequences of their vote. Fred Thompson is a pretty smart guy I must admit and he really cares about the people in Tennessee and I think Bill Frist cares too, but these guys are rich and stand to make lots of money after they leave office. Hell, I'm glad Senator Salazar won over Pete Coors. What was Pete Coors interest in government anyway? Legislation to affect the drinking age? Who knows? I do feel in my heart though, that our Congressional members are more out for what's in it for them than they are for their constituents. Year after year while I served on active duty, I had to watch the military receive pay raises of 3% or less when Congress would vote a pay raise for themselves in excess of 30% in some years. Something's wrong with this picture. If anything comes out of you reading my book, I tell you, go to the polls and stick it to every politician. Send the world a message that we're sick and tired of the games being played, the long term "heavyweights" in office who are self-serving and tired of the poor being taxed to death. Hell, gas has now reached $4 a gallon and even higher in some parts of the country! Minimum wage is only $5.75! Again, I ask you, what's wrong with this picture? We are being gouged to death, taxed to death and living in poverty while our politicians worry about "perks" and rides down the Rhein River! They have been self-serving for over 22 years now or at least during the time I've witnessed the "boys" in office. If I had my way, I'd love to see all women in Congress! Maybe we would get something done in legislation with crimes against women and children. It's a man's world and while I don't want to be sexist, I can't help it. The guys have made a complete mess of this world. I actually liked Nancy Pelosi, Senate Minority leader, standing up to George Bush! About damn time he's called on the carpet – that arrogant SOB! He hides behind his religion, but I guess God showed him that Mother Nature is in control. Mother nature will always be in control and I think he should be humbled that the world came to know that so many poverty-stricken people in the richest world were not cared for in the biblical sense. National pictures of people in body bags on the side of the road, left to rot like garbage for over a week is not what I call a "Christian thing to do." My God…what dignity did we give to those dying people? Spending resources to look for the living…give me a break. They were dead "black people" on the side of the road and Americans will rationalize that not only will they be better off after the hurricane because they're "used to living like that" but they have condoned the body bags laying over the streets. I can assure you had an earthquake hit the richest part of California; those bodies would have been placed in refrigeration trucks even as they searched for the living.

Chief Justice Rhenquist gets the flag ordered at half-staff after his death, but the tragedy that struck New Orleans never as much received that distinction. The President set aside September 16, as a national day of Prayer and Remembrance. In John Stossell's words, "Give me a break." Our leaders should have ordered the flag at half staff immediately after hurricane Katrina and ensured it remained at half-staff, until 30 days after the last body was found. On September 11, 2001, the President ordered the flags at half-staff immediately. A city in our country is submerged underwater and we pay tribute to the Chief Justice. I'm so sick of the big boys in Washington, D.C., patting each other on the back, telling each other what a wonderful job they are doing. The President praised Michael Brown on national television for doing a great job. Again, "Give me a break." I would have kicked his ass on national television and said to him, "Do anything and everything, but save lives now!" The President of the United States should have stepped in that dirty water. After all, his hands are stained with so much blood between the Iraq war, September 11 and now Katrina.

Imagine the President of the United States sat in a kindergarten school talking to kids even after his people told him a plane had struck the World Trade Center. Some people actually applauded President Bush for remaining in the classroom stating that this was a mark of a strong leader. I guess that's precisely why he is in office I am not. Hell, I would have stood up and said, "Hey kids, something really important has come up and I have to leave right now, but thank you for having me." The first and foremost job of the President of the United States is to protect the citizens of our country. Once again, it's my opinion, his lack of leadership led to two other planes slamming into buildings. He may not be an action officer, but he could have ordered the planes down. You cannot convince me that a pilot in his right mind would slam into the world trade center – that incident was clearly a terrorist attack in my mind. I thought then, that the President would order all planes down as a result. I thought wrong – it took too much time to make that decision. When Katrina struck, our President was on a five-week long vacation in Crawford, Texas. I'm telling you, the Bush family knows how to vacation. His father spent quite a bit of time fishing in Maine...the American people got what they asked for when they voted him in for a second term. I don't mind saying here and now, "I proudly voted for Kerry and Edwards." It's so unbelievable that our leaders in Washington have lost touch with poor and middle class America. Why should I be surprised? Wasn't it the first George Bush who couldn't quote the price of a loaf of bread?

While I'm on my political soap box, I may as well say, ever

since I heard the first George Bush make the statement that the people in Arkansas, "were the lowest of the low," while he was running against then, Governor Clinton, I lost respect for him. After all, President George H. Bush was the President of the "lowest of the low" and I didn't see him doing much to help Arkansas, but recommend that Eaker Air Force Base be placed on the base closure list. When I realized his son was running for President, I thought to myself, "George W. Bush ate at the same table as his father. He's most likely a chip off the old block, so he won't get my vote." His brother Jeb seems to have a lot more sense about him, but the dynasty has to end...people have to be smart. It's just too much power for one family.

CHAPTER 11

GRACE

Another few months have passed before I picked up a pen to begin writing again, but this time I think I can complete my thoughts. It's April 2, 2006, and this past week has been quite tumultuous. I've been feeling very anxious the past month, in large part due to Memorial Day fast approaching, the number of flashbacks I've been having and the personal stress in my life related to Grace. All of this came to a head late last week. I had finally made a decision to face one of my worst fears about two weeks ago. At my friend, Karen's request, she urged me to call Grace. I had not talked to Grace in over two years, I believe since I made my trip to Sedona, Arizona, in 2004. I accepted employment with the Department of Homeland Security just before my trip; however, I wasn't due to begin work until November 7, 2004. In any case, I decided to give Grace a call and tell her I was coming home. Of course, I got the answering machine again and the very sound of hearing her voice made me feel as if I was 30 years younger. There has always been something in her voice that stirs my inner being and I feel comfortable when I hear her. It wasn't until she retired that she decided to record a phone message. I'm not sure why but it just worked out that way. In my phone call to Grace, I informed her that I was happy to hear her voice and that I've decided to finally get in touch with her after all these years and literally face her in person. I told her that I would call her everyday until she picked up the phone or until I saw her. Again, no response and no returned phone call. I can't say I blame her; after all, there may be so many reasons why she never picked up the phone, but none of which she has ever disclosed to me. A week passed and I was leaving messages now, everyday around the same time. Typically, I leave the house at about 10:00 a.m. so that would be noon in Connecticut. I would leave a message telling her how beautiful the mountains were, how beautiful the sun was, how much the snow fell and then how quickly it melted. In between the phone calls, I continued to wonder, "Was Grace sick?" I worried about her because I have this connection that I can't even begin to explain. Well, I will explain or at least try to explain. Hopefully, you, my reader, will get the big picture.

One evening recently I awoke to a voice saying, "call me" in the middle of the night and the following night, I kept hearing "ALS" over and over again. I have "ALS." Why should I be worried about Grace's health you're thinking, right? I did and I needed to for my own health and my own life. As a result, I decided to tell Karen, my friend, about the dreams and that's when she said, you need to pick up the phone. Even at work, I explained to one of the other Transportation Security Administrative (TSA) officers while I was reading our standard operating procedures (SOP) in the training area. As I explained what happened, I began crying. For the first time in 23 years, I told some of my history to virtually a stranger. By the time I finished a brief synopsis, I had the Transportation Security Officer (TSO) crying right along side of me. I did what Karen asked and for nearly two weeks, I made a phone call everyday.

At times, I would search the Internet trying to grasp onto anything that might give me a clue as to how Grace might be feeling. For some unknown reason, I began to search "Poetry.com," looking for anything she might have written to me over the years. I searched on her last name and sure enough, plenty of poetry came up under her name. As I read some of the work, I came across some of the poems that I just knew she had written – possibly under a pen name because, after all, she was an English Teacher. When I began reading some of the poetry, I began getting upset. There were two poems I just "knew" she had written and I began crying. I was searching and crying.

It's unbelievable what these last two weeks have been like for me. Each morning I would jump out of bed, search for another poem and then run downstairs and read them to my sister, Karen. I'm sure she thought I was delusional but when I read her a couple of the poems, she told me, "Anything is possible, it could be."

A person with PTSD will grasp onto anything or anyone to keep them alive, to keep them feeling good, to take away the pain, to feel anything about themselves inside. We live in a state of numbness for most of our lives, or at least for those who fail to make an immediate or even lifetime recovery. We isolate ourselves from the world, we shut everyone and everything out, except those to whom we draw a close bond and trust. That's what I did for years. Not even my siblings were aware of the torment, the trauma, the separation of my body I felt when my military experiences grasp and took over my life after October 23, 1983. Not until last week!

In the meantime, the VA had finally got my "health buddy" in after waiting for it for nearly five months. The "health buddy" is a little white box with four buttons on it. I had to connect it to the phone jack and set it up. The first night I set up my "buddy" I couldn't get it working. I got frustrated with the thing and wanted to throw it on the floor, except my rational side took over and I figured the VA probably paid a lot more for it than the Air Force once paid for the $500 toilet seat, so I wasn't going to own a $3,000 machine, at least not yet. I finally got the thing working and answered a few questions. The next morning, I called my VA counselor to see if they got my responses and she didn't. Apparently, the "buddy" was a day behind. I'm getting to like my little "buddy" though. I come home every night looking forward to answering my questions, looking forward to the next trivia question or thought provoking quote by some famous person. This little "buddy" is my suicide watch buddy. So many people with PTSD never make it, they want to move forward but they, like me, are "locked in time." This disease just consumes you if you let it and I'm not going to let it. As I said, I'll do anything to stay alive and I'll fight this everyday of my life because life is worth living, no matter what you have been through.

Meanwhile, my sister, Karen, saw how much pain I had been in because she had never really saw it close up before. I'm living with her now and have been for the last six months. I think, with good reason, she was beginning to worry about my health. One morning, I told Karen, after not sleeping, that I made a reservation to fly back to Connecticut and see Grace face to face. I wanted to face her and tell her how I felt. Karen said, "Why don't you end it with her, just give it up, Bonnie?" "I can't," I said, "no one understands it but Karen, my friend." All these years, I've never told my sisters or brother for that matter, the deep connection between Grace and me. I never told them what happened to me in Germany. For all they knew, I was a lesbian in love with another woman, a woman I have loved for most of my lifetime. They found out this week though, the real story. Why I never shared my life experience with them, I don't know. I think I tried a time or two, but no one really listens. They hear what they want to and then they make a quick assessment. For all they knew, I went through a horrible experience and I should have put it behind me a long time ago and for some reason I couldn't. It's never that simple folks, remember that.

People with PTSD have a deeper side to them, a dark side often, a side that consumes their life and everything around them. One day, just one day, they learn to deal with their trigger points, they learn avoidance but some never learn how to deal with the pain. Hanging on to that pain helps too. It helps with guilt over not being there, over buddies being left behind, over not letting go because maybe you will forget and forgetting, while it's something one would like to do, you typically can't and so there is guilt over trying to forget. It's a cycle, like a snake trying to swallow its tail over and over and over again.

After I told my sister I was going home to Connecticut and that I had already made the plane reservation, she said, "Good, get it over, face her and tell her what you have wanted to tell her all these years." "Personally," she said, as she got up from smoking her cigarette while sitting next to the hot tub, "I would knock on the door, have her open it, and I would reach back for the door knob and say, 'goodbye' and shut the door in her face." It's not that simple and I knew then my sister had no understanding whatsoever why I was making this trip home. I said, "Karen, I want to be able to let go, I want to be able to move forward." Karen said, "To me, it appears that she's a cold hearted bitch. Why hasn't she just picked up the phone all these years to tell you to 'go away', 'stop calling me' get out of my life?" "I don't know," I said. "She's a part of this roller coaster I've been riding all these years and maybe she is afraid to do that." Karen said, "Maybe when her mother dies and she finds it convenient, then she'll have you."

Wow, my sister had no clue but she saw I was in pain. Somewhere between that morning and my pain, Karen must have decided to call my sister, Robin, in Connecticut. The two of them conspire in different ways sometimes. In fact, my three siblings have always felt a need to drag me out of stuff without consulting me. I remember a time after my father passed away and my family talked, without me of course. The three of them felt that it would be a good idea for me to take my mother and have her come live with me. They did this without discussing it with me first. I remember receiving a call from Karen while I was living in Tennessee and she said, "Now that Dad has died, we have been doing some talking and we think that you're in the best position to take care of Mom. You know she needs someone to watch over her and I can't do it because I'm married to Jack and in no way will he agree to having Mom live here with me. Robin is married to Caesar and has young children and Tom, well you know his situation with Linda. Mom and Linda won't get along and it's not good for them to have Mom there, especially having issues with their daughter Tammy right now. So we all talked and figured you should take Mom."

Amazing how "we all talked." Hell, I was never involved in the conversation. I would have taken my mother any day, even without them consulting one another, but now it was the principal of the decision. My siblings' decision to exclude me resulted in my placing a call to my mother. At the very second she answered the phone, I said, "Mom, Karen, Robin and Tommy are talking about you coming to live with me now that Dad's gone." "What," my mother said. "I don't need to go anywhere." I said, "Right, Mom. I agree. You know I would take you in at a moment's notice but hell, you and I both know you might start living again now that Dad has passed away. You can do things you wanted too and couldn't with him. There is no one to tell you how much money to spend on a dress or you can't buy shoes for yourself. I think it would be good for you to balance a checkbook, go to the grocery and shop, and start friendships with people you want too. Go to church, get involved in activities and really live." She said, "I am and I like it here. I'm not going anywhere."

What my family didn't know was that my partner, Kay, and I had already decided we were going to build a home for ourselves and give Kay's farmhouse to my Mom. In this way, she would live next door and I could see her everyday. I wanted to see my mother everyday and I wanted to take care of her. I wanted her to have some fun in her life. I wanted to take her traveling with us to places she never saw. How I would have enjoyed taking my mother around with me. I loved my mother as much as I loved my son, Jason, and more than I loved Kay. I spent so many years traveling around the world in the Air Force that I was looking forward to spending quality time with my mother, but that wasn't to be. On May 18, 1992, my mother passed away, six months to the day my father was buried in Dunnellon, Florida. She died of congestive heart failure six months after she had part of her lung removed as a result of cancer. My father died of lung cancer too. I was horrified when I got the news from my brother. To this day, I don't even remember how I got to Dunnellon to attend my mother's funeral. It was, next to the Beirut Bombing, the worst day of my life. I felt robbed of everything I ever wanted – time to be with my mother. She was so young, too young to have died. I never got to build that house, never got to take her anywhere, but Kay and I did spend the last Christmas with her and that made her very happy. Kay and my mother sang songs long into the night and it was indeed, a Christmas I will remember for my lifetime. We had such a good time. So, with that said, I wasn't consulted by my siblings. In fact, I was told this is what I would do. They soon got calls from my mother, I'm sure. They always mean well, though. I understand them, but I can stand on my own two feet. Well, I can't say that now – look at where I'm living – with my sister Karen and her partner, Chris, because I can't stand on my own feet. So that's why I'm not going to blame them for making the call to Grace.

I had made my usual morning call to Grace but this time I had written four poems for her that morning, March 31, 2006. I called her to tell her that I had written four poems. Shortly after, I was upstairs in my bedroom and as usual, I took the cordless phone up with me. I was in the middle of typing my poems when I received a call. I looked on the phone and saw that it was a blocked call, but even more I had this strong, very strong connection that that caller on the other line was Grace. Much to my surprise, it was because when I answered, I heard this voice on the other line ask, "Karen" and I said, "No, this is Bonnie" and I knew at that moment, it was Grace. I didn't connect the call as to why she would be asking for Karen. I simply figured she wanted to hear my voice and disguised her voice so that I wouldn't recognize her. Amazingly though – I did!

Anyway, I got dressed and went to the post office to mail the four poems I had written.

Later that afternoon, Karen called me, sometime around 2:30 p.m. on March 31, 2006, and said, "Oh good, you're home. I need to talk with you, I'll be home shortly." All the time I figured Karen was getting ready to tell me that she and Chris talked and they wanted me out of the house. Lord, I thought to myself, "Was I ready to leave?" No way was I ready nor could I financially meet my obligations if I did move out. Now I was getting more frightened. If I lived out of my car, I would never tell anyone, but that's where I would be if I weren't staying with Karen and Chris. I had a great paying job in Tennessee, but my stupid decision to leave it for "Monster" Michelle really cost me financially. I waited for my sister, Karen, to come home. My heart was pounding because I knew I couldn't make it on my own, yet I also knew that I wanted to leave more than they ever knew. Can I make it on my mere salary alone? I asked myself questions over and over in my head. I put Lady up on my lap for comfort. I grabbed a blanket and wrapped it around me because I was getting chilled. My body chills when I begin to get an anxiety attack. I thought to myself, just wait and see what it is she wants to talk with me about. Karen's never called me at home like that so it must be important.

The garage door opened and I waited in anticipation to hear what she had to say. Lady barked as Karen came in. I was sitting in the chair and she headed for the kitchen. She looked at me and smiled and I said, "What – you and Chris want me out now." "No," she said, "It's something else." I felt somewhat relieved. What news could be worse? She wasn't crying so I knew no one had died, so it couldn't be all that bad. Little did I know!

Karen looked at me and said, "Robin called Grace and Grace doesn't want to see you and said if you step one foot on her doorstep she is going to call the police." I can't tell you how outraged I was at that moment. My two sisters had violated my personal space once again, but in matters they knew absolutely nothing about. I guess they must have timed it right because Robin called Karen's phone or Karen had dialed Robin not knowing what I would do or say. In any case, Karen gave me the phone and Robin was on the other line. I was fuming, absolutely fuming. I grabbed the phone, while holding it in my hand, I shouted, "Karen, I'm going to kill you for this." Robin was on the other end saying, "Bonnie, you don't understand." I said, "Robin, I don't want to talk to you" and she said, "Who me?" and I said, "Yes" and hung up. She called back and said, "I heard you threaten Karen and if anything happens to her I am a witness." Now my sisters have lost it. I wonder who belongs on the psychiatric ward of the hospital now? I never meant I would kill my sister. I wouldn't harm a tiny little hair on any of their heads but I was angry and I cried and cried and cried until I couldn't speak. Karen put me on speakerphone and I tried to explain to both of them that they didn't understand. Robin proceeded to tell me that Grace was frightened to death of me and that I changed after the Beirut incident. It's all a blur to me right now, but I saw my opportunity to meet Grace face to face and meet one of my worst fears – the ability to let go and my sisters just took that right away from me. I began telling them how my mother and Grace were the two people that just happened to be in my life while I was in Germany that I clung too. Oh…I'll have to finish tonight because I'm off to work now. I don't want to get anxious about this because speaking about this makes me cry and sometimes it's so difficult. It's sufficient to say that I had the "catharsis of my life" and my sister, Karen, was present to witness it.

I guess at this point, I'll insert my last letter written to Grace on March 30, 2006, and a final poem to her on March 31, 2006. I think you'll get the picture.

Some of my letters and poems written to Grace

Dear Grace:

I never meant for you to be afraid of me…but I figured you might be frightened, that's why I sent you a four-line message through classmates hoping you might have dinner with me in a neutral place – with you driving and me following behind you in a car. I figured if I really remained outside your doorstep you would call the police… or better yet, you might hurt me because you were afraid. I didn't know what to expect really. Please don't ever worry about me taking my life, hurting myself or anyone else for that matter. I learned two years ago, after my treatment in the

95

VA, holding what I feel inside is more harmful than communicating. I spent the better part of 20 years not communicating any of my trauma to anyone except you and it nearly brought me to the edge of Pikes Peak. If not for a near blessing sent from God and Santa Claus riding in a Red VW next to me...I know, that sounds absolutely absurd, but Santa Claus has a Red VW with HO-HO1 on a Colorado License plate. (Long story, you wouldn't understand).

Until today, neither of my sisters knew the real depth of my pain, the separation I had from my body during the Beirut experience – Yes, Grace, I changed from that time. Tell me what soul on this blessed earth would not have changed? Tell me how many tears you would have cried and how you might have handled it. I handled it in the best way I knew how. I once told you that you didn't even know that you were there in my time of need. You were there by circumstance. People with PTSD isolate themselves and attach themselves to one or two people that they love and trust. My mother was one person and you, were the other. My sisters knew that – but Robin and Karen didn't understand the true depth and I really believe now, that you didn't either. They just believed I was "in love with you" based on what happened years ago. Yes, you did touch my heart with a simple kiss – and I emerged a more enlightened woman, though knowing who I was all along – something I've told you repeatedly to never blame yourself.

My trip home was simply to "let go of you" – let go of my pain, thank you for being where you were even when you didn't know it. Thank you for being my lifeline all these years. While I hang on to you, I can never let go of my pain. Keeping my pain keeps me in touch with all those

Marines that died so senselessly for our country. Giving up that pain and grief meant giving up on them. I understand I will live with this the rest of my life but anything...ANYTHING I can do to let some of my inner pain go – I WILL. It's no wonder you fear me, how could you understand. How could anyone understand unless they experienced death on such a massive scale themselves? I said I would walk into eternity with you because I felt like our souls were connected and yes, they are connected – I have absolutely no doubt about that. Dig deep into my poetry, beginning with "YOU ARE THE HEART OF MY OCEAN". I am in the "thawing out" stage of PTSD...although it took nearly 23 years to get to this point...and it is the beginning. My love for you has never been sexual.......never. In fact, I get sick to my stomach thinking about it, truly. I wanted to crawl in bed and hold you...just hold you – because to hold you would be to hold myself...that which you 'symbolically' hold...a part of me – the me that became separated from myself nearly 23 years ago. I asked you to take a trip to Tennessee a long time ago – to take your Mom along (to help you feel safe), to do just that...hold you so I could hold "myself". I offer you my life (that which you unknowingly hold) so I can move forward. Keep what you must...I entrusted it to you nearly 23 years ago...you've held me in safekeeping. I trust you will continue to do so.

I've met someone whom I really do love, someone I want to share the rest of my life with. Meeting her made me realize how much I needed to "let go of you." She knows 'everything about me and my life' but I was too frightened to make a real commitment to her. Letting go of you would mean I can move forward. I wished I could write poetry to her like I can for you – but I still have trouble with that because the part of me that writes poetry does not live in me – it lives in you. So I am writing poetry for me... Again, it's too difficult to explain to anyone......because it's simply unexplainable. I want to move forward again, hence, I sent you that letter telling you all about my past. I told Karen, my friend, that I asked you to 'tell me to come back to you and I will' or 'give me your blessing to move forward' and rightly so, she was upset. We talked more and she understood. What I really wanted you to do is to "tell me to leave" – "let go – it's okay." I know I don't need your 'blessing' – hell, I do what I damn well please. It just would have been good for me to hear it. But in your silence you refuse. I'm not about to change you Grace, nor would I ever expect too. You are you and I am who I am...but in my mind and in what's left of my heart, you still have a part of me living inside of you. As a result, Karen encouraged me to call you everyday until you answered...its no wonder you're thinking I've lost it. It's so not typical of me – but then again, moving forward from having PTSD in never "typical." I figured – you might just pick up the phone and I could convince you to have dinner with me – even lunch. All these years, I suspected your silence meant that you loved me and didn't want to let me go, why else wouldn't you have called to have me stop – but I never ever felt like you didn't understand me. I was soooooooo wrong. How could I have thought you understood? You merely feared that I might do something to harm myself or harm you, so you kept quiet and silent – which for me was actually worse than you telling me to move on. How sad...how awful for both of us. Yet you were also sacrificing your own pain and feeling afraid, by reading or not reading everything I sent you through the years, just to be sure I wouldn't hurt myself. Again...how very sad and how sorry I am for making you feel that way.

I was feeling good and you were in this state of compassionate torture. Unbelievable. I'm responsible for what happens to me. I can say, though, you're not responding kept me in the time warp – kept me locked in time – kept me from healing much sooner. Look for my book Grace – "Locked in Time" – you will see it published, be certain of that now. Thank You!

I'm debating where some of my proceeds should be distributed but I think the VA might be a good start.

I want nothing to stand in between my relationship with Karen as it did with Kay. That's simply why I was making the trip home. You always surfaced somehow in my life at the most difficult times…and of course you would. On Christmas, New Year's, Thanksgiving - the holidays, like Memorial Day, when we remember…and remembering is what I wanted to forget. So I got in touch with my "other self" – you – an extension of me and even though the communication was one way all these years, I was satisfied to write you – but to know that you were alive was more important to me. I received one card and one phone call in 20 years – why should I have expected more? I wanted to know not that you were physically alive but rather the part of me that still lives within you. (It's crazy for someone who doesn't understand – but not to me – not to Karen.) I never shared any of this with Kay – the true depth of my real pain. She lived with an empty shell, a broken body, a lost soul, and she tried to mend the pieces, but part of the puzzle was missing. Part of me was missing. Part of me was still residing in you and I didn't know it until after I left Kay and sometime after September 11, 2001. I think I explained that well in a previous letter. As I said, I was emotionally shut down, numb to the world, numb to anything and anyone, except you and my mother. I was even detached from Jason...poor Jason. I think he understands me...but even the part about my life in Germany is painful for him. He cannot speak about it to this day because he knows it causes me so much pain. When I lost my mother – it was another great loss, but one each of us will go through in life. If you don't know that loss already...you will one day and I pray that you will find a sense of peace from your mother's passing. I've always believed we are not human beings having a spiritual experience – we are spiritual beings having a human experience – that eases the pain I feel about death – at least for me. I've stepped into three funeral homes since Beirut – first at my father's death, six months later, at my mother's death and a few years later at my Uncle Jakes funeral. Shortly, I will return to see my Aunt Ruby, but I will not step into another funeral home – for it is in living that I must remember.

So periodically, I wake up at night – have flashbacks, remember Germany, remember the Marines, remember all that I did to care for them – to return them home to their loved ones, pieces shattered, lives shattered and I helped pick up the pieces, I helped wipe the sand from their hands...the sand that flows through that hour glass...the sand embedded into their skin, the stench of decayed body parts, maggots eating at their flesh, liquid pouring out from their legs, feet and hands dropping off into my hands – and I remember – and I reach for the pen and paper, jump on the computer and draft another letter to you. It's a cycle – like a snake trying to swallow it's tail – over and over and over again.

Suddenly, my body wants to thaw out – wants to heal from

all of this and move forward. I thought I needed to see you to move forward – but I don't. You're alive, I'm alive and that's all that matters. No more phone calls, no more letters, no more poems, no more need for you to fear me – as I stated before – you never asked to be put on this roller coaster – it just happened. I will live, Grace, without having to see you – I don't need to thank you in person. I don't need to tell you I love you – you already know this because part of me does dwell inside of you. (Then again, the 'you' really doesn't know this).

I'm not upset with my sisters either. They love me with all of their heart, and they simply want me to heal so they called you. If anything came out of this – they understand me better now. They don't understand why I never shared the deepest part of me with them, though. Why I never told them this connection with Beirut. Robin was truly awakened by all of this. The connection finally hit her...smack – right in the face. People don't listen...really. They hear what they want to. It's not fear of silence – it's fear that no one is listening. Poor Robin thought I was so obsessed with you over the years...loving you, missing you. There's a difference between obsession with a person...and being obsessed to find "oneself again". I grasp at anything that can help me deal with living...whether it's writing poems, letters to you, or just taking time to smell the beautiful roses, watch the sunset, look up into the stars at night while sitting in the hot tub, listening to beautiful music, or sleeping to make the day go by more quickly.

Time is said to heal everything...I completely disagree. Time heals nothing – Love heals everything. Until I met my current partner, I never truly knew what it was to have someone love me so much and understand me so well. I'm healing because of her love for me. We are in this together and I'm coming down from that roller coaster, slowly – but I'm coming down. She will have all of me... unconditionally and I will love her with all that I have and am capable of having.

I'm sorry you had to be put through this – I'm so sorry that you felt frightened of me all these years...nothing I can say can take back that hurt...but I am not sorry for loving you, nor will I ever be. For it's in loving you – that I can continue to live – because one has to love themselves in order to love another.

I hope this letter puts to rest everything you have felt over the years, everything you ever feared, everything you thought wrong and now is made right...it should have been said a long, long time ago. But then, I've only just begun to "thaw out."

Always and forever, with a heart of love,

BJ

THE HEART OF MY OCEAN

You are the heart of my ocean
Your very existence keeps me alive
Nothing else around me seems to matter
I'm holding on to this feeling – so fearful of letting go

Time seems so endless and yet I know the clock is ticking
The waves cover me – the water pounding against my face
The pain continues, relentless in the effort to arouse me
Vivid memories rip at the very core of my existence
Why can't I forget?

Then I reach down – deep into my heart
I'm reminded of you again
Nothing can hurt me anymore
For I have given more than I have left
And that which remains is all that I have.

You are the heart of my ocean
When the sun sets and the ocean grows calm
And you lie down to rest
I will close my eyes and rest with you
For all that matters will be no more
Why? You are the heart of my ocean.

By
B.J. Tierney
December 31, 2001

Written for
"Rose" who wears "Big Shoes"

(Note: I had asked "Grace" to send me a copy of this poem I wrote to her in 2001 and no response. However, recently I had Sarah, a friend of mine, who is renting my home in Tennessee, go through a suitcase that I left at the residence. There was a copy of my poem inside. I'm glad I kept a copy because I think it's one of my best poems...I wrote it during a very heart-wrenching period in my life. I gave "Grace" many nicknames throughout the years...Rose and Emily were just one of many.

IT MAKES SENSE NOW

Oh my God, I thought you understood
All these years
Why I have cried so many tears

Why I chose to keep in touch
Why I chose "not to touch"

You are but a spirit to me
Someone I've chosen not to see
The day will pass when you will know
My pain is PTSD.

Fear nothing from me
My eyes are open now
It's time for me to heal
The process has been long overdue
I will never blame anything on you

You have been my lifeline all these years
Many times you wiped away my tears
I'm saddened that you should have been afraid
It makes sense now.

You will always hold that key
I'm so sorry you were frightened of me
I'm not sorry for loving you
Nor will I ever be.
For it is in loving you
That I can continue to live
For it is in loving you – that I can love me.
They call it – PTSD

Written to Grace
Bye –
B.J. Tierney - March 31, 2006

ALL I NEED

My body is shaking
I feel chilled from the wind.
The coat that covers me is your love
It's Gods gift to me from heaven above.
I feel warm now
Thinking about you.
I can't remove my coat
Each season I wear it to keep me warm
It feels so good – the coat of many colors.
Brown – to remind me of your beautiful eyes
Red – to remind me of your ruby lips
Green – to remind me of your old "Camero" ☺
Blue – to remind me of the skies we once walked under
together.
Black – to remind me of your shimmering and shiny hair
that "Freddie changed"
Silver – to remind me that we're getting older and wiser
White – to remind me of purity – to remind me of my love
for you.
The coat that covers me is ALL I NEED
To keep me warm.

Written for Grace

By
B.J. Tierney
March 30, 2006

WHERE EVER YOU ARE

Wherever you are, I'll be there
In spirit, we are connected
Two souls dancing in the wind
I'll be there for you until the end

The sunshine on my face
The rainbows coming out from grace
The stars so bright
Shining long into the night

Everything of this earth
Reminds me of your birth
A blessing from heaven above
A blessing for me to love

Wherever you are, I'll be there.

Written for Grace

By
B.J. Tierney
March 30, 2006

WILL WE EVER...

Will we ever look out at the ocean and see whales jumping
up high

Will we ever see a reflection of the sun shimmering on the
water?

Will we ever smell beautiful flowers and watch rose petals fall

Will we ever watch the sunset sitting on top of a mountain?

Will we ever walk barefoot on a beach under a full moon?

Will we ever hold on to one another and never let go

Will we ever wipe the tears from each other's eyes?

Will we ever laugh with each other until it hurts?

Will we ever sit and share a wonderful dinner

Will we ever share stories late into the night?

Will we ever, ever, ever be _ _ _ _ _ _ _ _

Written for Grace

By
B.J. Tierney
March 30, 2006

I arrived home last night late after work, it was April 4, 2006, and as usual, I got this strong feeling that a package had arrived from Grace and sure enough, I went into the laundry room and sitting on the washing machine was a box postmarked to my sister, Karen. Inside the box was a letter from Grace addressed to both my sister and I. I took the box into the living room and opened the envelope, reading first, the letter written to my sister, and then read the letter written to me. I think I was motionless because the past days events had drained me so. I'm used to being numb to the world and holding my feelings in. I never even cried reading the letters. I'll share them with you now.

30 March 2006

Dear Karen,

I just finished talking with Robin. <u>Thank God</u> you guys got in touch with me. I have been going through a personal nightmare with Bonnie's obsession with me....which has <u>escalated</u> in the past few weeks.

Her delusions of an unnatural closeness to me and even my Mom really materialized when she had to process the pieces of Beirut soldiers shipped to her unit in Germany. I haven't written to her in years, maybe decades, but every so often a card or letter arrives showing an anxious, scared Bonnie....or, once in a while she calls. I have told her to not even contact me if she thinks I am her "secret love". And, for years, she obliged. BUT, I had no idea what was going on in her mind. For a long time, while she was with Kay, I rarely heard from her, other than their annual Christmas letter.

However, her insecurities obviously prevailed, and her miseries seemed to progress big time after 9/11. I dared not to draw a line in the sand and say "ENOUGH" "LEAVE ME ALONE" because in every phone call she sounded anxious, agitated, sometimes unhinged and somehow there was something about me or Rockville High (from the 70's) that made her feel safe for a year or 6 months.... I did not want to push her over any psychological edge she might be close to, if you know what I mean. And I **had nowhere to turn.**

I have sent along 2 packages she recently sent me. I do not want them...have not opened them. Attached to this letter to you is a letter to Bonnie. I ask that you read it yourself, first, and then, please read it Bonnie. I give you permission to read it to her. I hope that eventually she can find peace of mind I believe that life has been extremely disjointed for her maybe therapy or hospitalization can help her forget the pain of whatever is deeply disturbing her. Wishing you luck in this very difficult situation.

30 March 2006

Bonnie——

I am sending this letter to Karen and asking her to read it to you so that nothing is misconstrued, misunderstood or misinterpreted.

While I wish you all the best of good health and happiness, I must ask you, AGAIN, to stop writing to me and calling me about this delusion that you have of me. I was one of several teachers who was a friend to you and your family——nothing more. I am not any of those people you write to me about and address in your letters——I was once a friend——that's all. Not your "special friend" or "secret love". Your calling me and threatening to call me everyday until I call you, and then following through with it, is nothing short of harassment.

I tried to be an anchor for you during the really unfortunate and sometimes horrible experiences in your life, especially while you were in Germany and the Beirut bombings occurred. God knows, you have seen atrocities that few other humans have. But meanwhile, you were weaving fantasies in your mind about us. I warned you to stop; that we had a friendship....period. So, you fell in line, or so I thought. I have opened your letters because I did care about my friend Bonnie and her news of her son Jason. But, things slowly began spiraling, down and away, and you lost touch with the notion of friendship and became obsessed with fantastical thoughts about me. Your obsession seemed to magnify after 9/11.

The delusion must stop. You must get your life in order. You cannot dwell in the past, back in the 70's. Let it go! It was a safe spot good memories, but the REALITY is 2006 I know you know you must step away and move forward. You have certainly demonstrated you are a survivor. Do whatever it takes. You can do it. Let your family help.

Time to move forward, BJ. No more gifts, fictitious "us" letters; no more phone calls. Do not try to contact me in any way. And do not come here. There is nothing to settle because nothing ever existed between us except a friendship. All things must come to an end, and this obsession of yours has unglued that friendship. Your insistent harassment of daily voicemails for almost 2 weeks as well as a deluge of cards have scared me, shocked me and I am actually terrified by your threat to fly here and demand to see me and sit on my doorstep until you get your way that's stalking.

Please, stop.
Get on with your life. Grace

Hi Grace:

It's me again...your buddy, your friend, your secret love, your wandering soul mate, your nimwit, your everything that you want me to be, your inner voice sometimes, your memory, your guilt, your angel (well, I'm certainly no cherub :.)), your imagination, your fantasy, your light and yes, sometimes your darkness, your tears, your heartache, your joy and your laughter...and oh, how I love the very sound of that laugh and the sound of your most precious voice. It warms my very depths of human body and touches my spirit deep within. I just am. I am your beginning and your end...just as you are to me.

Laugh with me Grace, laugh with me today and always. Time continues and so does my deepest love for you. You have so many questions unanswered as I. Somewhere between those questions lie the truth, no games, no pretense, just plain old truth.

I know that you loved me and that you still do. You may be angry with me because just as I can't let go of you, I believe in my deepest heart, you can't let go of me. I'm not trying to play with your heart or your mind. I recognized this long ago. I struggled, of course, to come to grips with everything, beginning with my recognizing who I am, not "what I am," but "who I am." That recognition began a very long time ago, with me taking a long journey, loving three of my English Teachers, all in different ways. Each of you provided me a stairwell of opportunities to explore my inner self. Everyone departed, except you. As I climbed the top of the stairs, I realized who was waiting for me, whose hand I wanted to touch mine and that hand was yours. It's been my lifeline all these years that I have known you.

Your simple touch, your tender kiss, your eyes looking into the depths of my soul – you know me and I know you and our heavenly father from above, makes no mistakes with his creation. My love for you is not wrong. Everything about us or that has been about us is sooooooo right. You walk with Christ, I know that…and you are never alone. My walk with Him has been a long windy road and he still has plans for me. Your heart doesn't belong to me as mine belongs with you. Your heart belongs to Him. You've walked well in life, and sometimes, I'm sure it has been lonely journey for you. I've filled my void and emptiness with others. That little black book is really filled with just one name – yours. The truth is: I love you and would have become a nun, taken a vow of chastity, just to be able to see you every day in my life. My relationship with you is simply built on love.

Throughout the years, I have had relationships with a few people. What I call relationships is more than just sexual. There was Andy of course…and from our love came Jason. I knew about me long before you ever kissed me Grace, so please don't bear any guilt over what transpired. I believe I fell in love with you at the first sound of your voice as I walked into your English room on that September morning in 1970. There was Lynn, my first female experience. That experience was, of course, crazy. Sleeping with the maid. Oh, what we do to retaliate on "cheating husbands." Another relationship was Melinda and Kirk Crutchfield, former military officers. Yes, I cared about Melinda, and Kirk was more than happy to share his wife for her happiness. You know what? Years later, I realized I was just a toy, a plaything to make their marriage better. I was looking for more… a love that would replace what I felt for you. They knew you and how much I loved you. Today, you'd be happy to hear that this year, Melinda and Kirk will be walking with Christ as they join the Catholic Church this Easter. I am happy for Melinda because growing up Jewish, she really had no foundation for religion nor a relationship with God. Having to admit to one's sinful life is not easy, but even worse is not confessing one's faith in Christ. I'm sure the Bishop got an earful but I'm also sure God has forgiven them.

In between Melinda and Kay, there was a woman looking to find someone, but no one even touched my love. They were sexual encounters. Then there was Kay...my ten-year partner. She used the love I had for you to capture me. Everyone knew you...everyone feared you...because they knew they never truly had all of my love. They had a piece of me, but you had the deepest piece. Kay basically used me to get to where she needed to be – in her retirement. She was good to me in many ways, but I was vulnerable at a time in my life when I should have been strong. I used her too. After all, how can one truly love someone fully when they love another? She knew that, accepted it and we remained together for ten years. I couldn't open up to her and let her in. How sad for Kay. I left emptiness with her because I couldn't be there emotionally for her. It's no wonder she found it necessary to look elsewhere. We were great friends and companions and still remain in touch. I left that big house on the lake too, signed a quitclaim deed, just as I made Andy do for me. The difference, I gave up my part of the house to Kay and made Andy give the house in Merced to me. I even left many of my belongings and antiques I purchased while in Europe. There is one thing I left with – my sanity and my dignity. I always proclaimed I was faithful to her and I was. I could never look at another woman. I would never be unfaithful in my relationship.

Still, I was, because I loved you. I probably would have stayed with Kay the rest of my life, but I also knew I couldn't.

Then came Michelle – the awful mistake of my ever-living life! God help me for getting involved in that monster of a situation! God did help me actually. He lifted me up and brought me back to those beautiful mountains in Colorado. To this day, my personal belongings remain in a storage facility in Arlington, Virginia. I pray, one day, I will be able to get them out and move into a place I can truly call home. When I came to Colorado, I first lived with my sister in Littleton. Then after looking for a job for nearly eight months, living off my savings (what little I had after spending), I sought treatment in the VA facility. It's actually humorous that while staying on the Psych ward of the VA hospital, I got an interview with 'lousy' 7-Eleven. I went to the damn interview in a beautiful business suit and my hospital band on my right wrist. Can you imagine that? They probably thought it was another 'colorful' bracelet. The next day, they offered me a position for 46K and 15K bonus to become a field consultant. I moved to Colorado Springs and rented a room from Elizabeth Thompson. Funny. I lived on Rockville Drive of all places. She rented a room out to me. She had more boyfriends than the stars in the skies. I always looked forward to her next story. Of course, I told her upfront that I was gay…and guess what…she too knew of you. She cried with me one day, saddened that I should have loved someone so long and be so heartbroken. She tried to get me out to do country dancing, but all I did was work and sleep. I worked for 7-Eleven about three months before there was a shooting outside the store. Lord have mercy! I decided that managing 7-10 stores in very bad parts of town wasn't for me. More important, I thought I would die for my country, but not 7-Eleven!!!! I quit the next morning. For the first time in my life, I could walk away from a job and tell them to take the job and shove it right up where the sun doesn't shine. I felt soooooooooo good doing that!

Two weeks later, the Department of Homeland Security called me to work at the Denver International airport. It was then I decided to take my trip to Sedona working my way down past the International Balloon fest – September 2004 and the last time I called you.

I moved back to Denver and rented another room from an Italian lady and Customer Service Rep for United. Now this lady was "Whacko," but I didn't know it until I moved in. Her name is Dona Rigatto, people call her "Rigatto." It's hard living in one room after having a full home. I still have the house in Tennessee. My friend from Kelly Services is renting from me – thank God. (*Note: At the time of editing, I've had to put my house on the market for sale. Sarah managed to get a promotion and I'm happy she did. It's about time for her to get what she deserves, but I'm wondering now, how I'll make the payments until I sell the house?) I don't want to go back to Tennessee though…sometimes I miss it because the standard of living is much lower than in other parts of the country. The mountains in Colorado are too beautiful for me to give up at this point. I rented a room from Dona for over nine months. She wanted a friend and a companion to do things with, but all I wanted to do was sleep, eat and work. I did just that. I was the perfect renter. I would come in, go to my room and sleep. I'd wash my clothes and go to work. She wanted someone to watch television with…I watch very little. I think she wanted a friend – I'm not sure. I just wanted my space. And – you've heard the reputation of the flying industry…well it's true. She had been married and I guess her husband turned out to be gay. She couldn't understand why. Hell, if I were married to her and I was straight…I'd be gay too! HA! You have to understand Dona.

While I was in Colorado Springs, I gave match.com another try. After nightmare Michelle and the mistake of my life…I said, "Someone is out there and I hope that someone is you." I put this crazy profile up – my screen name: "BigShoes4Me." Oh, I got responses all right. I got responses from some real looney tunes. One though…caught my eye. The person who responded appreciated the depth of my comments and I agreed to meet her. It turns out she was a Catholic woman, divorced from an Army Major. She had been in an abusive relationship with him. It also turned out that we were both from Connecticut, she lived in Rocky Hill and we graduated high school the same year – '73. We played basketball together and her father is buried in the same cemetery as my grandmother and grandfather. We met at a diner. When she stepped out of her car, she was holding a cane. She could barely walk. I later learned that she had been in a very bad car accident. We have been friends now for over one and half years. Her daughter is a news producer for NBC news and her son is a banker. When she responded to my profile, her own her profile said she was looking for a man? I wrote back and said to her, "Do I look like a man?" I think you've made a very big mistake lady…a very big mistake. I later learned that she didn't want her daughter to know about her desire to be with a woman. Wow – and did she pick the wrong woman to contact. The most 'out lesbian' on the face of the earth! HA! Just joking. I do like to keep my life private of course, but in my own home with the person I spend the rest of my life with (or hope to spend the rest of my life with), I will not make any pretense.

So darling, this has been my life. I suppose your next question, "does my friend know about you?" You bet she does. She knew about you the very first week. She's tried to get me to consider changing my "Classmates.com" profile, as well as, my profile on America online (AOL), but I told her, I can't because the deepest part of my heart belongs to Grace. She said she is willing to have a relationship with me full well knowing how much I love you. I haven't made her life easy, but I truly feel she understands me and you know, I do love her. She's committed to me in every way. I don't want to end up in another situation like I had with Kay.

I cannot walk into eternity with anyone else --- but you. That will happen without you having to say you love me. I want more though. I want to see your smiling face more often, have dinner with you, maybe take a trip together. You need not fear me, Grace. Just feel warm by knowing someone loves you and has loved you forever.

Tell me to come back to you – and I will. Tell me to move forward and give me your blessing and I will. Just stop running from me and let's move forward. No regrets from the past, just recognize what we have between us and move forward. I wanted to share all this with you, not to hurt you, but to demonstrate what has been happening to me. I wished you would have moved to Tennessee and lived next door to me! I'd be the happiest woman on earth. I could have been your next-door neighbor seeing your smile everyday. I can't cook, so you'd starve and if you have a weight problem like me, that might be good for both of us. We could go to the movies together, have hot chocolate on a cold morning, travel together and if you are ill, I can help you, be by your side and take care of you. You know what? The only one in my life I ever wanted to care for is "YOU." Everyone else gets mad at me because I have little patience for their sickness. That's weird, I know. I never felt that way about you when you got ill. I wanted to be with you – send you flowers, help you through difficult times. Everyone else – I want to kill when they get sick.

If you want, you can remain my secret love…write your poems to me, tell me how you feel and I will be your sounding board. I will keep my distance – but I will never ever lose my love for you…NEVER. I am not angry anymore because I do believe God makes everything right and perfect. My love for you is absolutely perfect. You only have to look at my smile and my eyes to know that!

Today, when I called you…just hearing your voice again lifted me – it choked me up too. You can mist my eyes so quickly. You are the very air I breathe everyday. Please know that and please know that when heaven calls, for either you or me, we will walk into eternity! I beg of you, please let me gaze into your eyes once more…let me touch your hand, let me hold you tightly, let me feel our hearts beat together. Do not fear me Grace – I will never break your heart again and no matter what you say – you will never break mine no matter what you tell me. My love is a blessing and what I feel for you is too. You may feel I am playing games – I'm not. That would be your great loss, to move into eternity and feel like everything has been lies and deceit. I've just never known how to tell you the deepest truth and I was overcome by fear of rejection. So, I got into one relationship after another. How much I have wasted my life.

I once offered to take you on a cruise – I once offered you a trip to Tennessee – I once offered my hand. Now I offer you my life. I do not want to wait until heaven calls...I do not want that to be our home....not yet!

You are so very precious.........a beautiful rose in full bloom. Let no more pain pass between us, let's just live today. Do not cross that bridge Grace...to Heaven's door...I simply want more time.

I remain forever,

Your buddy

Those are just a few of my letters more recently – I lost most of the letters I wrote to Grace over the years. The letter above was written before my last letter. My writings are pretty pitiful actually. Don't feel sorry for me either, after reading some of these letters. I just hope "Grace" will understand that I included this personal information into "Locked in Time" because, for my own recovery, I need to do so. I am moving forward and I'm so very sorry she feared me.

CHAPTER 12
GET ON WITH YOUR LIFE

PTSD can grab hold of an individual and affect him or her in so many different ways. I understand why Grace thought I was some crazed woman in love with her and well, I won't deny I cared about her; but even I am trying to make sense of everything. I want to finish my book. In reading the past chapters, I hope you understand what I have felt over the years and maybe a bit of how I am feeling now. For those of you who study PTSD or treat patients with PTSD, then you will have insight into the mind of someone who has had this disease for a very long time. More importantly, my book is directed to those who may suffer or think they suffer from a traumatic event. Please get in touch with yourself and seek help if you are experiencing some of the same symptoms I have experienced or described. **"YOU CAN'T GO IT**

ALONE" – no matter what you think, **"YOU CAN'T GO IT ALONE."** You will end up some statistic like our Vietnam War buddies, with more of them committing suicide than died in the Vietnam War. I understand why, but I also understand that while living can be painful, it's possible to learn to adapt to our environment and it's possible to learn to "love life again." I've missed so much through the years letting this disease take hold of me...I want my life back, I want to move forward. It's time, as Grace said, to "Get on with your life."

Tonight, one of the top officials in the Department of Homeland Security was arrested for Internet porn and trying to contact a 14-year-old girl. Why are so many men lurking to commit such indecent acts upon children? It's time women take a stronger role in Congress and enact laws that are harsh on sexual predators. We have too many men in Congress making the laws. I'm happy they caught this guy. I know, if I were elected to Congress, I would enact tougher laws because, in my personal opinion, it's only when you have been abused do you understand the importance of such laws. I really admire Oprah for making child molestation an open issue for discussion on national television.

A week has passed and all I did on my day off was read and re-read Grace's letter to me. I was hoping she might have opened my last letter to her but if she did or didn't, I will never know because I intend to obey her wishes and never contact her again. When I wake up at night now and have those nightmares, when I am haunted by the memories of the past or have difficulty coping day to day, I will turn to the computer and write my thoughts on these pages. I would have had ten books written by this time had I written down all my thoughts and letters over the years. There is something different about writing to an individual to whom I felt connected rather than just writing my thoughts down on paper. Everything is inside and soon I will share more and more of myself.

Am I delusional as Grace indicated in her letter? I wonder. I think I'm an individual who is in great pain, who has experienced a trauma like none other in my life and I am trying to pick up the pieces and move forward. Every once in awhile I will get a note from someone who knew me, either another Air Force individual or someone from high school.

I created an album on Classmates.com so that people could see some of my photos and get in touch with me if they wished and today, I received a note from Robert Perkins, a former non-commissioned officer (NCO) I was stationed with in the Philippines. It was so refreshing because he made such a kind comment about me being one of the nicest and kindest people he ever met in his Air Force career. He doesn't know it, but his comment lifted me in this difficult period of my life. He was there during my difficulty with Andy, my ex-husband. Amazingly, he is here now again, touching my life in just a little way. Bob was funny and a good NCO. I worked for him when I was enlisted at Clark Air Base in the Philippines. We both worked in the Intelligence Division under lock and key. I remember one time the Intelligence Division was broken into. This place was supposed to be secure, but apparently it wasn't. We had all our Secret documents behind lock and key, but Filipinos broke into the office and stole my typewriter. They sat around and drank all our soda from the refrigerator and took all of our personal belongings. The next morning when I walked into the office and found my typewriter gone, I worried how I was going to get my work done. Bob just laughed because, well, after all, we were the government, not private industry. That same day, I got another typewriter. Back in the 70's, we had those "Selectric" typewriters, the newest ones on the market, and I'm sure they were expensive. The Filipinos like to break in and steal things when they could. They didn't make much money over there and selling government goods was how they made their living.

Each night when I closed the office, I left a note written in Tagalog that said, "Please don't take my typewriter." Guess what? They broke in again and left another soda bottle on my desk and a note saying – "No problem – you can keep your typewriter."

I understood Filipino (Tagalog) and I think the locals respected that I did. I learned that my husband was cheating on me by secretly learning the language and Bob Perkins helped me get to the bottom of it too.

One day, I sat down with Bob and begged him to help me with my marriage. I said to him, "I think Andy is cheating on me again and I need your help to find out so I can end this terrible ordeal." Bob asked me "What do you want me to do?" I said, "Let's plan a trip to Manila one weekend with you and your wife and Andy and me. You talk to Andy and see if he's cheating on me and then let me know." I begged Bob to help me. He agreed.

We went to Manila one weekend as I recall and had a great time seeing the sights. We stayed at the Manila Hotel and went out to dinner. I don't remember much about that weekend, but I do remember the purpose of the trip. I returned to work that Monday and Bob came into my office and he said, "Bonnie, what are you going to do with the information I tell you about Andy?" I said, "Bob, I just want to use it to make my decision to leave him. Please, tell me what's going on with Andy?" He walked back to his office and I could see he had a worried look on his face. I followed him and I said, "Please Bob, tell me." He said, "Yes, Bonnie, Andy is cheating on you. In fact, he's so proud of it that he even offered one of the girls to me if I wanted to mess around with them." I remember my heart sinking to the floor and I felt so humiliated. I lifted my head up and I looked at Bob and said, "Thank you, Bob. I know that was hard for you. Thank you." "You're not going to do anything crazy are you?" Bob said, as I turned to walk back to my office. "Of course not," I said. I went back to my office, stayed about another 30 minutes and watched Bob walk up and down the hall. He was obviously worried and having second thoughts about telling me about Andy. Finally, I felt this rage consume me and I just couldn't hold back my emotions any longer. Within seconds of Bob walking down the hall in the other direction, I jumped out of my seat and left the office and drove home.

When I walked into the house, Andy was lying on the couch. It was his day off and he was watching television. He liked watching the local Filipino comedy shows. He was wearing his usual white tennis shorts and T-shirt. I remember the surprised look on his face as I walked in, but I passed him and said, "I need to get something upstairs that I forgot." I walked into the bedroom and went to the waterbed headboard. It's where we kept the gun in the house. It was a rifle, a .22 I believe. Let's just say it was a gun, something dangerous. I pulled it out and then began frantically looking for the bullets. In every drawer I searched, I couldn't find the bullets. To this day, I thank God I couldn't find the bullets because I was capable of murdering Andy for what he did. This wasn't the first time he cheated nor was it the first time I felt humiliated because of his proclivities. I held the gun tightly underneath my right arm and walked down stairs.

I walked over to Andy with the gun in my hand and I pointed at him and said, "You son of a bitch, you better tell me the truth. Have you been cheating on me again?" He was so frightened as he should have been. I had the gun pointed right to his head but only I knew there were no bullets and the gun wasn't loaded. He lifted his head from the couch and I said, "Don't even think about getting up. Tell me, is it true?" Andy looked at me, laid his head back down and said, "Yes." I can't remember what happened that made me lower the gun but I felt so horrified that this could happen not once, not twice, but the third time in our relationship. I guess Andy saw I was vulnerable because he jumped up so quickly, grabbed the gun from my hand and threw me into the chair. I told him it wasn't loaded and that I wanted him to move out immediately. I told him it's over, no more chances, no more us. It's over. Who was I kidding? I knew it was over after Jason was born and after I had an affair with Lynn, our live-in servant. I was angry at Andy for cheating on me so I was going to get back at him. Was I any better than Andy? I do believe; however, had Andy been more attentive to me, more understanding, more loving: I, too, might not have searched elsewhere for intimacy. I don't know why we do what we do, but it was over. I can't remember if I ever told Bob that I took a gun to Andy and would have killed him had I found the bullets.

At that time in my life, I knew that everyone was capable of murder given the right or wrong circumstances. Since that time, I realized I was capable of murder and I also realized that taking someone's life is not the answer. **Another life's lesson learned. "Don't ever take a gun, even jokingly, and think about taking someone's life. It's never worth it – Never!"** Thank you, Bob. Thank you for being there at a difficult time in my life.

CHAPTER 13

I STILL REMEMBER

I have so much on my mind right now. I'm avoiding paying bills, doing my taxes and thinking. When I get in this mood, I just listen to soft, relaxing music. It's not working tonight though. I'm so depressed and my stomach aches from all this pain. It's like I've been run over by a truck. Tomorrow is another day and while I have an agenda, I wonder, will I leave the house?

I just wrote another poem this morning, feeling motivated again. The pain continues after another night's sleep or should I say after another sleepless night. I'm so drained over the past week's events. So very drained. I'll share it with you.

I STILL REMEMBER

When I raised my hand and took my oath
I could have never known
The land I loved with all my heart
Would send me far from home.
There across the ocean nearly 23 years ago
In a land so far away
My life suddenly changed in just one day.
Soldiers upon soldiers
One by one they came
In black body bags
Some just in pieces
Body parts covered in dirt and soil
From terror in a land so far away
Handle them gently and love them greatly
For they died in their sleep
So senseless they died for no reason
In the fall of the season
They spoke to me one by one:
I am in heaven
Take what remains and honor me, but weep for me no more.
Like you my solider, we always stand at death's door.
I took my oath to honor and obey
Now, strength and courage is yours to display.
Weep for me no more.
Though I was sleeping in the barracks that night
I would have rather had a chance to fight
But terrorism is a coward even in the darkness of the night.
The battle will continue my friend
Your life will be changed forever
For on this day you send me home

You will always remember.
Weep for me no more
You now have to struggle each and every day.
I wish with all my heart I could take your pain away
But I know I cannot
Weep for me no more.
Return me to the land I love
To the country that I served
Please honor me in a way I deserve.

Nearly 23 years have passed and I still remember
The 241 Marine soldiers who died and went home in November.

By-- Bonnie J. Tierney- Written - April 6, 2006

I received a message in my email this morning from Lynda Green, one of my classmates from Rockville High School. She was asking me if I remembered James Sloan, one of our former classmates. I sent her a quick note to say that I did. In fact, I could never forget Jim. We both were in Mrs. Hyder's eighth grade English class at Sykes School in Rockville, Connecticut. How could I ever forget Jim?

I believe it was the fall of 1968 when I was assigned to Mrs. Hyder's English Class. I could never forget that day I walked into her class either. I always arrived first, typically, or at least up until the time I walked into this class. I remember taking my seat in the far right hand side of the room. I sat facing the entry door in the first seat, second row. The reason I remember where I sat was simply because as people began walking into the room, I noticed that I was the only female in the class. I kept looking to see if someone other than myself would walk into the class. Much to my surprise, I was the only girl in the entire class. Talk about feeling different! Actually, I didn't, but I thought to myself, "How can someone make such a mistake?" Mrs. Hyder walked to the front of the class and I quietly leaned over and said, "Am I in the right class? Are you Mrs. Hyder?" She smiled and said, "Yes, you must be Bonnie." I leaned back in my chair and remembered thinking; "You've got to be kidding. This is going to be a great year. I'm in here with all these guys and this is great." She asked me if I felt uncomfortable and wanted to be sent to another English class and I said, "No, why should I be uncomfortable?" Most girls would have wanted to run and hide, but not me – because I wasn't like most girls.

Rockville High School administrative officials soon came to realize I wasn't like most girls. In fact, I was like no other they had seen. I was progressive and I was a feminist. Long before Gloria Steinem burned her bra, I was a feminist. After all, I had been raised on a farm and my Uncle Jake made no distinction between what guys and girls did when it came to work. We worked equally and were paid equally. Now he was progressive. Certainly, he was the most influential male in my entire life. I loved my Uncle Jake for so many reasons, but mostly because he treated everyone fairly and with respect. Well, sometimes, not everyone was treated nicely. Maybe I should share some of my stories about my Uncle Jake. After all, he was a very big part of my life and the positive force for much of my success.

CHAPTER 14

MY UNCLE JAKE – MY HERO

Y ou've read previously that I liked to wear my Uncle Jake's clothes and nearly got my father in a tizzy over finding my Uncle's pants on my parent's bed, but what I haven't told you was that my great Uncle Jake was my "Hero."

Uncle Jake was married three times. The first time he married was long before I was born. Apparently, he married a New Yorker for about a month or so. I suppose it was a big family secret because I never knew the circumstances surrounding that marriage until after I turned 18 years old. He inherited the farm from his parents at an early age and to my knowledge, he hated city living. He couldn't live in New York City so he ended up having his marriage annulled and moved back to the farm. Soon after returning to South Windsor, Connecticut, he married his second wife, Gertrude. Now she was someone I got to know and didn't like at all. To me, she was the wicked witch from the Wizard of Oz and she was mean as hell. What Uncle Jake ever saw in her will remain forever an enigma. My family never liked her and I believe the feelings were mutual. We were a poor family by New England standards. In many ways, Uncle Jake was kind and understood that in order for my father to get ahead, he would need to help our family purchase a home so we could stop renting apartments and settle down. Regularly, we worked on the farm, helping my Uncle Jake raise tomatoes. One day, Uncle Jake told my father that he would donate all his profits from the farm to my father so that we could have a down payment on our home. We finally had the opportunity to purchase a home and we have Uncle Jake to thank. Uncle Jake always paid each of us well. In the 60's, an eight-year-old kid making $20 bucks was unheard of, but he gave us each $20 bucks a day. I could share so many stories with you, many that would make you laugh, but what my Uncle Jake and I shared was special. He was Army Sergeant and it wasn't until he was 93 years old that I learned about his participation in the Normandy invasion. I always wondered why my Uncle Jake was cold and unemotional. We just chalked it off as being, "Uncle Jake." I realized years later it was the effects of war that caused him to be detached. He saw the unspeakable too. We had shared our experiences. He was a simple man and taught me well. We raised tomatoes and peppers on the farm and each year, we would open the field to the public to pick tomatoes. I would collect the money from the people and the first year I began collecting the money after his second wife, Gert, passed away, we collected about $800 on the first day. My Uncle Jake was so astounded by all the money I collected, that he gave me $100. He said, "I've never hit a day like this. I usually get $400 or $500 maximum." The next day the cars came into the field and again, I collected nearly $900 that day. He was shocked again and gave me another $100. By the third day I was outside waving cars into the field thinking, I'm going to make this the biggest day ever and sure enough I hit over $1200. When my Uncle Jake came home, my pockets were bulging with money. I couldn't find enough space to keep it all together. Here I was, just 12 years old and carrying around $1200. I was left at the house all day while he worked for Hamilton Standard in Windsor Locks, Connecticut. I think he helped make the "moon pack" for the astronauts that went into space. When he came home, I was so excited that I threw all the money on the kitchen table and said, "Am I getting another $100 bucks today?" He laughed and said, "At this rate, I'm going to give you $200 and then I'm going to pay you a normal days wage after this." In just three days, I made $400 dollars. How many kids do you know in the middle 60's who made that much money? Needless to say, my father took most of my money to pay for dental bills and then he made sure I knew that the money would also buy my school clothes at the end of the tomato season. Finally, my Uncle Jake sat down at the picnic table and said, "I think Gert and her mother ripped me off all these years. How can you collect all this money is just three days?" I said, "Well, I'm honest Uncle Jake and I would never take anything from you." I think he was disappointed to know that all the years that he let his wife and mother-in-law collect money on the farm, they were stealing from him. He smiled and said, "You can't cry over spilt milk." He taught me many life's lessons. One year when we had a storm uproot all the tomato plants, he looked out in the field and said to me, "One man's misfortune is another man's fortune." I said, "What do you mean Uncle Jake?" He said, "Well, take a tornado for instance. If the tornado blows down all the houses on the street, it's very unfortunate isn't it?" I said, "Yes, sir, it sure is. It's horrible." He then said, "Horrible for the home owners but for the builders, it's good." Then he went about doing his work to clear the fields for another planting.

My Uncle Jake couldn't have any children of his own and I think he felt very close to the "Tierney" kids, as much as we felt close to him. He was like a real father to me. He was my greatest teacher in life. He and I always had a strong connection. For those of you who may be non-believers, I must tell you that God works in miraculous ways. One particular Sunday, I was in church and part way through the pastor's sermon, I heard a voice tell me, "Go home to Connecticut, your Uncle Jake needs you." As the congregation stood to sing a hymn, I heard to voice once again, tell me, "You must leave and go home now." I excused myself by stepping in front of people and out into the aisle. I immediately went home and called my supervisor at ABB Inc, where I had been the HR Consultant in Alamo, Tennessee. I informed Carl Blackside that I needed to go home right away because I felt my Uncle Jake needed me. He had been ill and was under hospice care for quite sometime. I called Southwest Airlines and made my flight reservations to depart Nashville, Tennessee, to Hartford, Connecticut. When I called to obtain my ticket, the agent said, "I can get you on the next flight but it leaves in three hours." I told the agent to book me on the flight. Immediately, I packed a bag and took off to the airport. While standing in line in Nashville to check in, I heard a voice behind me, it sounded like my brother who lives in California. As I turned around, I saw my brother standing in line about six people back. He caught my eye and we both said to each other almost simultaneously, "What the hell are you doing here?" I said, "I'm flying home to Connecticut to see Uncle Jake." He said, "I am too." He jumped up to the front to stand next to me and we both got on the same flight. He said that our younger sister, Robin, was picking him up at the airport. I said, "Good, she can get me too." When we arrived in Hartford, Connecticut, we immediately went to my uncle's house. My Aunt Gert, (his third wife) and the most loving and beautiful woman you would ever want to meet in your entire life, met us at the door. She informed us that Jack, as she often referred to him, was in a coma and on heavy morphine. She walked us into the room and there in the hospital bed, lay my Uncle Jake. There was a white sheet on top of him and as we walked in the room, my brother said, "That's the death rattle." I looked at him and of course, he was referring to my Uncle's breathing pattern. My brother, sister and I stood around the bed and I said, "Uncle Jake, we've come home to see you. Tommy is here, Robin is with us and so am I. Everything is going to be okay, Uncle Jake. You don't have to worry any more, we're here to help take care of you and Aunt Gert." At that time, I laid my hand on his chest and my Uncle opened his eyes. He grasped on to the bed rails and lifted his head and looked at each of us. He smiled and laid his head back down on the pillow. We stayed with him until just before midnight and my Aunt Gert said this was the first time he had woken up in weeks. She said he was hanging on for some reason and I just said, "Maybe he was hanging on to see us." We then told my Aunt Gert that we were going to leave and we said our good byes. As I got in the car and we were driving to Robin's house, I felt this chill come over my body. I began shaking and feeling ice cold. With my brother in the front seat and my sister driving, I said, "Uncle Jake has just passed away." My sister, Robin, said, "You don't know that." "I do," I said. "I'm so cold and when we get back to your house, Lin is going to call and tell us that Uncle Jake passed away." We no sooner got in the house, the phone rang and it was my Aunt Gert's daughter, Lin. She told us that 15 minutes after we left their house, my Uncle Jake had passed. Believe what you may, but I am certain that I felt my Uncle Jake pass away at the moment I felt the chill come over my body. My Uncle Jake was my hero and will always remain my hero. After he passed away, Lin sent me his dog tags and a photo taken of him while he was in the Army. He was cutting a log. I laughed when I saw the photo because I did the same thing when I was a Captain in the Air Force. My, how time stands still.

Jacob Stone, my great Uncle, while stationed in Europe serving with the Army. (Pictured on the left standing and sawing)

Captain Bonnie J. (Tierney) Caceres, while assigned to Eaker Air Force Base, Blytheville, Arkansas, as the Director, Morale, Welfare and Recreation (MWR).

CHAPTER 15

ANOTHER TRIP DOWN MEMORY LANE

It's April 10, 2006, and I haven't been sleeping well this past week. I've been having some intrusive thoughts again about veterans and their service to our country. I awoke this morning to a stomachache and feeling a lot of anxiety. It didn't help either to have my health buddy ask me questions this morning instead of last night when I got home. I guess I'm feeling anxious again. It's a deep down fear I have that I might not make it to the end of this book. God, I pray I will make it to complete this endeavor. I don't want that little machine planting any ideas in my head. A few of the questions I was asked this morning was if I felt hopeless or something to that affect. I'm sitting in my "room" which is basically my little house in my little world and I don't see much changing. I'm not feeling sorry for myself but I am having this feeling like nothing is changing and I'm doing about everything I can to make it change. What I need right now is a good paying job that will satisfy my self-esteem. My stomach is really killing me. I think those questions bothered me - waking up to them. I usually want to begin my day in a good way and now I'm not sure if that's a good thing – making me think in this manner. I'm anxious and I want to reach for my medication to help ease some of this uneasiness. At the same time, I realize that the numbing effects of medicine are not good for me. I must be in the middle of another anxiety attack. I'm going to turn some soft music on and then begin writing again. I just need to relax. Last night before going to bed, I re-read Grace's letter to me and I kept wondering if she ever opened my letter. Does it really matter at this point? She wants to move on with her life and desires me to move on with mine. I kept reading the part about in my sister's letter that said, "I believe life has been extremely disjointed for her....maybe therapy or hospitalization can help her forget the pain of whatever is deeply disturbing her." Deeply disturbing me – you've got to be kidding. What the hell does she think is deeply disturbing me. How about 241 dead Marines? How about living with memories of them everyday of my life for the last 23 years? Is it possible I could be deeply disturbed by those intrusive thoughts? Hell yes. I dare anyone to live with seeing such atrocities as she called it. I feel like a survivor of the Holocaust, but then I can't even begin to imagine what those poor people experienced and went through. They were literally "walking around dead." Why can't we all just get along in the world?

Yesterday, while working at the airport, one of my teammates made the very same comment and I told him, "Now that would make a good book." We hear people say everyday, "Wouldn't the world be a better place if we could all just get along?"

Maybe Grace is right. I am disjointed and the way I am writing this book is disjointed too. All right then, all you medical professionals out there read this book and figure me out. I dare any of you to figure out PTSD and then find the ultimate cure. Find the cure for cancer too because it's similar. It destroys people, kills them almost like a flesh eating disease.

Where's my music? I left off talking about Mrs. Hyder's English class. She was a wonderful teacher and a good friend. She would help me both professionally and personally over the years and I feel much gratitude for having known her in my life. My high school years were very difficult and there were times I didn't think I would make it through but Linda and her husband, Rich, provided me a retreat, a home away from home. Years later when I entered the military I would call them just to touch base and see how things were going. I lost touch with them after my experience in Germany. In fact, I lost touch with nearly everyone in my life except for my mother and Grace. I lost touch with the world, too.

Did I mention earlier that Linda helped me with my English lessons after school? We were in Sykes Jr. High in Rockville, Connecticut, and Linda was teaching me some difficult conjugations. We spent about an hour each week going over the daily lessons and one evening after additional lessons, we left the room. Linda closed the door and suddenly there was this huge crash. It sounded as if the building caved in. We were both standing outside the room and we both heard the loud crash. She opened the door and we both looked inside and you wouldn't believe it, but the entire cement ceiling came crashing down on top of every student's desk in the entire room. To this day, I thank God no one was in the room and that we got out just in time. There's no doubt in my mind that we missed being killed together. Tons of cement came tumbling down and the only thing I could do is look shocked. I wrote a poem to Mrs. Hyder and I called it "Brown Eyes." She may have saved it. I can't be sure but I wrote about the "roof came tumbling down" and I think it was the very first poem I ever wrote. Now you know where my writing skills began. Sykes High School was very old and looking back now, I'm sure, in fact I'm certain of it; the school was closed because it was so old and probably filled with asbestos. If you believe in divine intervention, then you know that God waited for us to leave and better yet, for all the kids to be gone. I also remember a time in Mrs. Hyder's English class where one of the guys, Michael Tompches, a young boy, cute as a button, asked to take a bathroom break. He left the room and shortly after he left the room and in the middle of one of Mrs. Hyder's English lessons, Michael had apparently crawled up into the ceiling and decided to have a cigarette. How do I know this you ask? Well, the crazy fool got far enough out and over our classroom and fell smack dab down on the floor, while still holding his cigarette in his hand. I never laughed so hard in all my life. There was definitely something about those ceilings. I think Michael fell through the ceiling before the ceiling came crashing down. Michael sat behind me in English class and always flirted with me. I liked him a lot. He knew how to make me laugh. I think he hated that class, but I also think he enjoyed sitting behind me and tickling me too. He used to run his pencil down the back of my neck, scratch my back and twirl my hair. He definitely had heightened hormones. I remember him handing me a pencil one time, pointing out the name on his pencil: "climax." What a name to have on a number two pencil. Of course, Michael did everything in his power to show me the name on the pencil every chance he could get. His mind was on sex all the time. I bet Michael ended up being one of those "Chippendales." Whenever Mrs. Hyder began word conjugations he always loved the lesson on "lie the book on the table," "lay the book on the table." He was one of the only students in my high school years that could make me laugh so hard that I wanted to pee my pants. It was also a struggle to keep from laughing too because he liked to torment Mrs. Hyder. Her hair would get out of place as she ran back and forth from row to row trying to keep order in the class. I think those boys gave her a hard time on purpose. They actually loved messing with her. How she ever made it through that year is beyond me, but she did. Eventually, as I read years later, she became the head of the English Department. Linda Hyder deserved her success at Rockville High School. She was such a positive influence in my life and made a real difference. I'm almost certain through the years, she gave her heart and soul to teaching students. I'm almost certain she used her work to escape her own problems. She was good at hiding her feelings too. She learned the art of hiding early on in her career. Like so many abused women, she just kept it to herself and those close around her. She's a survivor too.

Yesterday while at work, I began writing an article I hope to have published in the <u>Rocky Mountain News</u> or the <u>Denver Post</u> during Memorial Day. The article is about Veterans, of course, and how many veterans fear Memorial Day. How can we make the American public understand that many of these holidays are difficult periods for veterans? Here's my first draft. Let's see if it gets printed.

"VETERANS REMEMBER MEMORIAL DAY TOO"

Memorial Day is just around the corner and the Veteran's Hospital will be filled with people visiting our soldiers, paying tribute to their service to our country. There is another group of people who will also visit our VA hospitals across the country too – The Veterans themselves. Not for the reasons you may think, though.

For many Veterans, Memorial Day is too painful. It's not just another holiday, it's a day in their lives they wish to forget. On Memorial Day, as Veterans, we are made to remember the dead and for those of us who have been diagnosed with Post Traumatic Stress Disorder (PTSD), we want to forget Memorial Day because we remember the dead everyday.

I served on active duty both as an enlisted non-commissioned officer and as an officer while serving in the United States Air Force. I'm considered a Vietnam Era, Gulf War Veteran. As one of the officers involved in the recovery, identification and processing of the 241 Marines killed in Beirut during the bombing of the Marine barracks on October 23, 1983, nearly 23 years ago, I have never forgotten. I will never forget but over the last few years, while receiving treatment at the Denver VA facility, I've learned to identify some of my trigger points and try as best as possible to cope by living in a world where terrorism is covered daily on news channels, in newspapers and in everyday water cooler conversations.

It was on Memorial Day, 2004, when I found myself engrossed in television coverage of the World War II dedication ceremonies held in Washington, D.C. Like many veterans with PTSD, I began internalizing all the pain again. As I sat in front of the television and watched for hours upon hours, I saw many veterans talk about their stories. These veterans also witnessed similar atrocities. I wondered if they saw death on a massive scale like I did. My Uncle Jake served in Normandy and it wasn't until he was near his deathbed that he disclosed his involvement in the Normandy invasion. For years, I wondered why my great Uncle was so isolated. I wondered why he couldn't show any emotion and why he seemed to be so cold and so hard. When I finally got in touch with my own feelings, I realized he most likely suffered from PTSD as well.

The pain grew hour by hour as I watched television during the week's events. In nearly 21 years, I talked little about my experiences. I wrote about them to a friend but even she never understood the trauma I experienced. Most people can't even imagine.

Suddenly, I grabbed my sister's dachshund, Lady, and jumped into my sports car and began driving. I wasn't sure exactly where I was heading but I knew I was going south. I headed toward Colorado Springs, toward Pikes Peak. As I continued to drive, I thought to myself, "I can end all this pain, the nightly flashbacks, the recurring intrusive smells of decayed bodies, all the things that reminded me of my duty as Mass Casualty Officer in Europe." Lady was sitting beside me in the front seat and I kept looking over at her. She is so beautiful and so innocent. I was innocent too. I was just a First Lieutenant in the United States Air Force and only 29 years old, like so many of today's soldiers, so young to be experiencing such trauma. Maybe if I had died I wouldn't have had to experience all this pain.

While driving on I-25 South towards Pikes Peak, I kept thinking, "It will all be over when I drive my car off the top." I kept thinking, "How many years have I lived with these intrusive thoughts? How long had I lived with a disease I didn't know I had?" I just knew that I never talked about my experiences while on active duty. I feared seeking help because I would be considered a weak officer and there was nothing more deadly to a woman's career on active duty than being a "mousy-weak" officer. I didn't want my medical records, promotion records blemished in any way so seeking counseling or psychiatric help was out of the question. Was I going to be another statistic? Another veteran who commits suicide because I can't live with my memories? I wonder if most people even realize that more Vietnam veterans committed suicide than died in the Vietnam War? Am I going to be another casualty?

I began crying and crying and tears began rolling down the sides of my cheeks. At some point, just prior to Pikes Peak, I looked up through my sun roof to the sky and said out loud, "Dear God, give me a sign to help keep me from taking my life. Help me with this pain, please."

No sooner did I ask God for help, I saw this red VW pull up along side of my car. I turned to my left to look at him. The man inside the car had long white hair and a long white beard. He saw that I was crying and I became embarrassed.

Veterans learn to hide their tears, many of them crying in secret. If veterans don't cry, then they drink, they go on wild spending sprees, overeat, take illegal drugs – they do anything to numb their pain. The guy in the Red VW looked just like Santa Claus. He kept riding along side of my car and I fought to hold back my tears now. I couldn't though, I just cried and cried. Suddenly, he lifted his right hand from his steering wheel and gave me a "thumbs-up" sign. He then sped up and passed my car. As he passed, I looked closer at his vehicle and his Colorado license plate read, "HO HO1. Could it really be Santa Claus? He was driving a Red VW too. He kept his distance but close enough for me to read the bumper sticker on the back of his car. It read, "Miracles happen everyday, Remember Christmas."

I got my sign from God at that very moment. God sent Santa Claus to ride next to my vehicle and I knew then, I would see another Christmas. I never drove up Pikes Peak; but I did turn around somewhere short of Pueblo. I passed Santa's village on the right and I made a promise to stop in and see if the man in the car was the same man who God sent that day. I drove back to my sister house and took Lady back inside. I thought about keeping my plans to commit suicide a secret, after all, only Lady and I were present. I couldn't keep it a secret though. I knew I needed to seek treatment.

The following morning, I told my sister, Karen, what I planned to do and she wanted to take me to the hospital immediately. I told her I would check into the Denver VA and begin treatment. As doctor Sturgis, my Psychiatrist, once said, "You're only half-baked after a very short two-week stay." I never got into the PTSD program at Denver because at the time, they only held classes for male veterans. Even some of my own horror stories bothered some of the Vietnam vets in for treatment. Sometime in the future, I'm supposed to attend a program in Menlo Park for women, but try to balance paying bills and a 90-day hospital stay. It's not easy. I can't afford to take the time off, yet I can't afford not too.

I'm almost certain there are other veterans out there who will contemplate taking their lives on Memorial Day too, so I just thought I would help educate the public. Memorial Day and often, July 4th are some of the most difficult holidays for our Vets.

If my article can stop one veteran from taking his/her life, and they seek treatment at the VA, then I will have accomplished what I set out to do in this article – Save a Veteran.

I extend my heartfelt thanks to the Denver VA for their continued support, helping Vets adjust with PTSD. Without their support, continued calls and monitoring, I would not be thanking them today. Each day is a struggle but life is truly worth living. Intrusive thoughts come and go and Memorial Day will come and go, too.

To the public: This Memorial Day do not only remember and honor the dead, but also remember those Veterans who are struggling each and everyday to forget. We have given our souls and many have given their lives so you can be free. So when you're out taking a walk and you see a man living on the street, don't pass him by. He most likely served his country. Stop and thank him…thank all Veterans who are alive…don't wait until Veterans Day. The public can make a difference. This war is wrong...terrorism is wrong but it's the price we pay for freedom. It's the price I've paid for nearly 23 years and I will never forget.

At the end of the article, I included the poem entitled, "I Still Remember" that I shared with you, the readers of this book already in the chapter with the same title. I thought this poem deserved to be printed.

CHAPTER 16
THE VA RED TAPE

Today is April 12, 2006, and I'm off for the next two days. I'm feeling very depressed at the moment. I just returned from another VA appointment. My doctor wanted to do a follow-up on the arteries in my neck. I had an ultrasound test completed this morning and at the completion of the exam, the technician asked me, "Do you have high blood pressure?" Amazing he should ask that question. I responded with, "No, but this morning I had another anxiety attack."

When I woke up this morning, I went downstairs to look through my paperwork and I remembered the Department of Veterans Affairs sent me a letter to reconsider my VA disability claim. I guess in the letter they were asking for additional information on my condition. Hell, how much more information do they need from me? It wasn't enough that I gave up 19 years on active duty, one year short of retirement. Even until this very day, I continue to live with this demon and memories of my experience while I was serving on active duty with the Air Force while stationed in Germany. Now, the regional office at the Department of Veterans Affairs in Denver, Colorado, wants me to dig up more memories and obtain letters from people who knew me. Dig up letters from people who knew me – are you kidding? People with severe PTSD rarely let anyone in and rarely do they let anyone get to know them. Of course, there was Kay, my best friend and confidant. I reluctantly picked up the phone to call her and ask for help, but I did.

I called Kay this morning to tell her that I needed to get a letter from her outlining my life with her and my everyday living experiences and difficulties she witnessed while we lived together. I asked her to explain truthfully, the difficulties I had with establishing intimate relationships, difficulties in my social life, difficulties with my work and my thoughts of suicide throughout the years. I had to painfully re-hash all this with her this morning and yes, if anyone would have high blood pressure over this, it would be me. We both cried on the phone and I tearfully told her that I was sorry for being so distant and so far removed from her. She in turn told me that she tried to make me feel comfortable, tried to show me love but that I never believed her. She even apologized for getting abusive in the end but that she too, was at wit's end with how to deal with me. After all, during the time we spent together, I refused to seek help and I figured the problem was mine and mine alone. How wrong I have been. I feel so sorry for the spouses and the significant others associated with the PTSD soldier. Life is truly a living hell. Talking to people with PTSD is like talking to the wall because we all learn defense mechanisms and we trust no one with our life, heart and soul. We get angry, we spend money frivolously, we get in and out of relationships, make hasty and rash decisions, are impulsive and most of all, we show very little emotion. All the time, we continue to cry for help and it's like no one understands or listens. We are our own worst enemy.

It's so hard to rehash these old wounds. I also told Kay about Grace and what happened with my sisters contacting her. She told me that I should have had Karen or Robin send the last letter because maybe Grace would never read it. Kay knew about Grace and the connection. I thought I never told her but I apparently did. I never dwelled on it though and maybe that's why I felt like I never shared it with her. Up until today, I had forgotten the time Kay and I were in the car driving somewhere, probably to Memphis, Tennessee. I remember telling Kay that I wanted to just live in the woods and be a hermit. I figured it was easier than living in society. I could hibernate and just go to town to get my food once a month. Never see anyone or anything and then I would never ever have to be hurt again. I also remembered telling Kay, as I held out my hand, as if to hold my "heart" in the palm of my hand. "It's all I have," I said, "Please watch over it and protect it. I can't stand to have my heart hurt anymore than I have. Hold it gently, Kay" I said, "Protect it with all that you have, because this is all I have left of me."

I cried so hard this morning that my nose was running and bubbles were coming outside. I began to read her the poem I wrote and the article I wrote for the newspapers to print on Memorial Day. I could hear her on the other end, crying too. Poor Kay, she's not well anymore either. She's had heart problems recently and she's not doing well. She told me she was fighting back pneumonia and it sounded like it. Kay was always the strong one in our relationship. She was like a bull. She was one of the strongest women I have ever known. Maybe, just maybe all these years since we have been apart, I was wrong. She did love me and I just never knew it or I tried to drive her away. I think that's it in a nutshell. People with PTSD and especially those of us who have been abused are more susceptible to failing in our relationships because we simply don't trust anyone. One thing I know for sure is that Kay understands me more than anyone. She took me when I was a broken and lost soul and struggled to give me a home where peace and serenity surrounded me. She helped me understand nature and get in touch with myself as best as she knew how. I was my own worst enemy. The more I sit here and think about my life – I don't think anyone understood me better than Kay. It's time for me to wipe my tears and get my haircut. I'm sure I will clean up well and pretend that today was just another day in the life of Bonnie Tierney. I continue to hide my pain and only will I let those I trust know.

Shortly before I got up to write the previous few paragraphs, I had thought again, "Why must I endure this pain?" I can make it so easy on myself if I just swallow a few pills. As I laid on top of my covers, I imagined my sister coming home only to find me in a pool of blood or just find me peacefully sleeping from taking an overdose of medication. I'm stronger than that though. I grabbed Grace's letter to me and I re-read it again and again. I'm not a stalker. I'm not any of those things she indicated in her letters. I am a veteran, a disabled veteran who served my country well. A person who experienced atrocities that she spoke of...but most of all, I am a survivor. I am a SURVIVOR.

I have to keep telling myself that I am a survivor. Kay always told me that you live what you think. She has never been wrong. I am a survivor. I'm a survivor of sexual abuse. I am a survivor of physical abuse and I am a survivor who has PTSD. Yes, indeed, I am a survivor.

I asked my sister today to draft a letter to the VA to support my claim as well and also talked with Kirk and Melinda. They too, agreed to write letters for me.

It's November 3, 2006, and once again, I put this book on hold. I have to go back now and see how many months have passed. I was told by my therapist to put the book on hold because it was stirring up too many emotions. Stirring up emotions is a good thing for me because I've kept my emotions inside for too many years. Still, I followed the advice of my counselor.

I just flipped back about a few pages and six months have already passed. I suppose I should believe it because a lot has happened in six months. At this rate, I'll have the book done at about 85 years old and then the people this book will matter most, won't remember anything anyway. Lord, I've got to do a better job at this endeavor.

It's 2:19 a.m. and as I look back, I noticed that I had stopped about the time I had to justify my rating to the VA for my military service connected injuries. I get so upset about having to justify my illness and I often wonder how do these Vietnam Veterans, especially homeless veterans, ever complete their paperwork. They don't I guess – they just survive day to day on the streets. I received a late notification the other day that my DRO (decision review officer) actually decided to rate my PTSD at 50% rather than 30% and my injured knee at 10%. Yesterday, I took sick leave so I could go up to the Department of Veterans Affairs and get my hearing rated as well. Now what boggles my mind is that the VA already rated me 10% on hearing, issued me two hearing aids about two years ago, but my rating was 0%. When I went for the exam, traveling nearly two hours from Denver VA Medical Center, the audiologist asked why I was there? She's asking me, "Why are you here?" "Hell if I know," I said. "I just received a call two days ago informing me to come and get a hearing test." I forgot to mention, too – I have changed jobs between the time I last wrote. Working for the Department of Homeland "insecurity" just about killed me. The worthless management about did me in. I had applied to an Administrative Officer's position with the Department of Veterans Affairs and was hired on June 11, 2006. What a miracle and how grateful I am to be employed once again with the government, but this time, for an agency where people truly understand veterans.

I received a notice to complete paperwork for my appeal to the Department of Veterans Affairs. The paperwork was sent to the wrong address and dated September 27. I actually received it about October 18 and thinking I had just 30 days to complete the paperwork, I went into another frenzy. It wasn't until I called the Disabled Veterans' of American representative in Denver at the regional office that I found out I had 60 days to appeal. More importantly, at that time, I found out the VA actually increased my rating from 40% (30% PTSD & 10% (what I thought for hearing) to 60% (50% PTSD & 10% for the knee injury I sustained while in Russia). When I was talking to the DAV representative, I was actually not feeling well again and I began crying uncontrollably on the phone. I explained to the DAV representative, who later identified herself as a retired Marine Gunnery Sergeant, that I was sick of all this paperwork and that the VA was now telling me two years later that my rating had been increased by the DRO (Decision Review Officer) before my appeal was decided. I told the DAV Representative, I hold a master's degree and even I don't understand all this paperwork. She informed me to wait until I received my decision from the VA and then make an appointment to see her. I agreed and I think that's when I hung up and thought to myself, "I could just end all this pain, frustration and suffering, just by walking into the bedroom and taking an overdose of my medicines." I thought, "If I just lay quietly down on the bed, take a handful of my Ativan, then I can go peacefully and I won't have to bother with this any more." I'm not sure what stopped me, but I do know I thought about it for the remainder of the week. I'm here still…so the reality is: I want to live but I want this whole process of justifying my illness to go away.

To make matters worse, I decided to go see "Flags of Our Fathers" – now that's a movie all Americans should go and see. I'm not sure about all veterans, but for those who can muster up the strength and go with a "buddy," I might suggest they go too. Although, after I saw the movie, I remember walking out with my girlfriend, Karen, thinking to myself, I've got to see this again. We do that to ourselves, those of us with PTSD. We punish ourselves by reliving bad experiences and internalizing the pain others feel. After the movie, I got in the car and was driving Karen back to the house and she said to me, "Why are you so distant now? Why are you moving further away from me? Is there anything I can do for you?" I wanted to say, "Yes, be quiet and let me suffer." I just said, "I need my space –

just leave me alone for now please." Realizing she really wanted to help me, I drove a few more miles until we reached the house. I was trying to figure out ways to go back to my house simply because I wanted to be alone now and go watch it for a second time. All the time, I was thinking that after the movie, I would go home, lay down on the bed and take those awful pills and end my life. No more memories, no more pain, no more reminders of my service to my country, no more reliving these awful events. For the first time, I shared my thoughts with Karen and I told her, "I need to stay with you tonight." I shared my thoughts and what I had planned to do. It's so morbid – why would I want to put myself through this show again? Why did I want to be alone? Why did I want to consider taking my life? Why, why, why?

I stayed the night with Karen in Colorado Springs and I was glad I did. I survived another day. I went back home to my apartment on Sunday, October 22, and then I realized – tomorrow is October 23. It would be 23 years ago that I was involved with processing the Marine soldier's body parts. I called in sick on Monday morning...I just couldn't face going into work. I called my VA telehealth nurse just to talk. I tried to tell her that I was punishing myself by going to the movie and having thoughts of suicide again. She said, "You shouldn't go to movies that remind you of the trauma, Bonnie." She didn't have to tell me, I already knew it. Still, it's like an addiction. There are some people who cut themselves to feel pain. I wanted to punish myself by seeing the movie again and again and again. I have to say one thing about the movie though. The average American citizen will finally "get it." They will understand the trauma of a veteran with PTSD by observing the life of Ira Hayes and the other veterans involved in Iwo Jima. A few days later, I remember also thinking, "I get it too." For the first time, I let go of the animosity I have felt toward the Lebanese people for the tragedy they caused. Somehow, the inner anger I felt toward them just disappeared. I no longer felt like killing every Lebanese person for what happened to the 241 Marines 23 years ago. What changed me?

Imagine living every day in a world where terrorism is a daily occurrence? Imagine you are a child, waking up every day only to see bombs exploding outside your home, seeing blood in the streets, watching parents carry their children to hospitals, seeing dead people bleeding in the streets, watching cars burn, seeing big gigantic holes in the ground. Imagine how your life would be affected. Imagine losing your parents to a suicide bomber. We can't imagine it because we are not living in it. If I, who spent just 30 days around dead bodies and body parts can be so horribly affected by what I witnessed, how much greater is the pain experienced by those who live it everyday?

I have since come to the conclusion that nearly all the Middle Easterners are suffering from some type of PTSD. How can they not? Knowing this sheds a different light on my own perspective and how I view things. I'm not trying to rationalize behavior, but I am saying that if the general American public would realize that living in conditions like this is so very harmful to a person's psyche, what is it that we need to do as Americans to help them overcome this illness?

For starters, we need to adopt a diplomatic policy. War is not working. Destruction is not working. Kindness will work. Compassion will work. Transforming lives by changing the environment will work. For generations to come, we have instilled in the young minds, revenge, hatred and retaliation for all that they have witnessed and the only way to overcome this atrocity now is to inculcate values of peace and compassion. It's difficult for me to explain this concept because for nearly 23 years, I have not had a forgiving heart. I too, wanted revenge. Revenge serves no purpose for anyone, especially not the "internal self." Revenge is like a bad worm eating your insides out. I have envisioned myself attending the 25 Anniversary of the Beirut Memorial Ceremony and visiting the second wall. I see myself purging and becoming very ill as part of my recovery process. I told my therapist I wanted to go to the wall and touch the names of the men who I helped put together. She said, "Are you sure?" I said, "Of course I am." She said, "Most people end up in the hospital after going to the wall." I'm sure she was referring to the Vietnam Wall. Still, each wall contains the names of dead soldiers. I have this need to throw-up because I think it's the act of getting all the poison out of my body. To me, it's the final act of ridding my body of every last bit of poison I have held in. It's time to let it go and I'm not sure what will happen after, but I do know I have to make that trip and find out. Now you understand once again, why I came up with the title, "Locked in Time.

I couldn't sleep last night and as it turned out, I woke up only to find out that Saddam received the death penalty. The judge ordered death by hanging. Saddam apparently became upset and said that only common criminals are hung and therefore, he preferred death by a firing squad. Amazing that he should want to choose how he dies. Karen called me to tell me about the sentence and she said, "He should die the same way he caused others in his country to die and that's by gas." I wrote a poem the night they put Saddam to death.

HEAR MY CRY

As we sit with baited breath
Waiting for the news of his death
I feel cold
Hear My Cry

Millions are speaking from their grave
"Let him take his last breath"
For we know the pain and suffering he caused
May you never forget.
Let him die…
Hear My Cry

Let him rest now let him be
Return him to me
In the ground dust to dust
Forget him now, you must.
Hear My Cry

Do not celebrate his death
But…remember me
For I too, suffered under thee.
Hear My Cry

AirForce1
Bonnie J. Tierney

The world may be a better place without Saddam, but to celebrate his death is so morbid.

One evening after watching Larry King, I saw Roseanne Barr giving an interview. She announced that she wanted people to join her on her website and make the United States a better place. I have to thank Roseanne for the many hours I spent on her website because she managed to get the creative juices flowing in me again. Since the time I joined, I also called for an American Summit and got people so motivated to do something about building America from within that she actually shut her site down for some time and then blocked me as a member on her forum. It wasn't until that time that I realized how powerful words can be. Still, she is doing wonderful things for Katrina victims and the effort to rebuild New Orleans by helping with her various fundraising projects.

In the last few weeks, Hillary Clinton made the announcement to run for President by saying she is "In to Win." When I look back through my manuscript and realize how much I have written and the content part of me wants to scratch out information and the other part of me is saying, "Hey, it happened." I spent a significant amount of my time blogging on different websites about the latest news. There is nothing I would like to see more than a "Hillary and Warner" ticket and what I have challenged Senator Clinton to do at this point is to select her Vice President right now. She should do something different and save lots of money. The money that politicians spend on running campaigns is so wasteful. There is no middle class any longer. Most middle class citizens are a paycheck or two away from being homeless. There are the poor and the rich. I wrote a comment almost immediately after Hillary's announcement that I was proud that Denver was selected as the great city to host the DNC in 2008 and that it would be known for "real change" for "real people." In another blog, I stated that I would open my home to one woman so she could attend the DNC and shake Hillary's hand when she wins the nomination. Her response to me was that she would never shake her hand and would spit on her shoes. I, of course, responded that I would certainly then "spit shine" Hillary's shoes. I followed with another comment by stating, "There are those in America who shine shoes and those who own shoe stores." We need a good team in 2008. If that 2008 team is: "Clinton & Clinton," "Clinton & Warner," or "Barak Obama & Warner" or "Edwards & Warner"...I will be a happy "Democrat."

CHAPTER 17

MY WISH FOR AMERICA

As I close the chapter of this part of my life, and step out from being "Locked in Time" and move forward, I do so as a result of many people who made a positive difference in my life. Many friends at Rockville High School in Vernon, Connecticut, and my classmates who continue to believe and encourage me to make that difference in the world. It would not be right if I did not pay tribute to former Governor of Virginia, Mark Warner, who never changed. His generosity and kindness brought over 70 of our graduating members from the Class of '73 together for a reunion in Richmond, Virginia. He is a man of moral character, concerned about the future of our country, concerned that our children will be educated, that our health care systems will benefit everyone, that family really matters. I look forward to Mark Warner picking up the gauntlet and running for office in the future. I look forward to a time when every America citizen can send their children to school, where everyone has a roof over their head and food on their table. I look forward to a new day…when the doors are opened and people in America really wake up and become active participants in the decision making process of placing great leaders in office and giving public trust to not those who are rich, but those who can win the people's hearts because they truly care about what happens to our citizens in America. I look forward to the day that no veteran who served will live on the streets.

I will visit the Beirut Memorial on October 23, 2008, on the 25th Anniversary and I will leave a signed copy of my book so that my brothers know – they did not die in vain. They will know on October 23, 2008 – I am no longer "Locked in Time."

This book is dedicated to the 241 Marine soldiers who gave their lives while serving their country in Beirut, Lebanon and to the many family members who lost their sons, husbands, brothers, fathers and uncles.

A few weeks ago, as I finished the final manuscript, I was corresponding with a former teacher, from Rockville High School, Vernon, Connecticut. I was relaying a message that one of our former classmates, Sara Humphry Lanciano, had died from ovarian and pancreatic cancer. I was distraught over the loss because it was just three years ago that we had our class reunion in Richmond, Virginia, and Sara looked so lovely and in good health. Sara will always hold a special place in my heart – for she was such a unique and beautiful woman. She had a rare gift of getting to know people, I mean really getting to know people. I remember telling Sara at the Governor's mansion, I had a "girls crush" on her in high school and she blushed and smiled. She actually said she was flattered and smiled again. You have to know Sara, I think she just didn't want to hurt my feelings. I will always think of Sara in a very special way. "Mr. Lav," as we fondly referred to him, also encouraged me to move forward, especially when I wrote to tell him I had completed my book. He said he had something to share with me about the Beirut bombing. I wrote back and said, "There were several Marines from Connecticut and I always wondered if one such Marine that had lived in Ellington, Connecticut, was related to Mr. Dick Tingley, a former teacher at Rockville High School." He was the school's football coach in the 70's. Many times I often wondered if the "Tingley" Marine was any relation to Mr. Dick Tingley. Mr. Lavatori wrote back to say, "Yes – the young Marine was Mr. Tingley's son." Upon reading the email, somehow I felt a sense of closure about that issue because I had never asked and I always wondered. In fact, who could imagine, miles across the ocean, that I would be involved in the recovery, identification and processing of those Marines killed and that one of the Marines who died in the attack, was the son of our high school football coach? As I recall, and my memory fades over the years, Mr. Tingley was our escort during my junior year when I took my first trip to Europe. We went to Spain in 1972 and I remember spending my college money on that trip. Now, nearly 24 years later, I find out that Mr. Tingley lost his son in that senseless bombing. I can't recall specifically if Mr. Tingley's son's body had been sent to Rhein Main Air Base, Frankfurt, Germany. It really doesn't matter at this point. What matters is that Mr. Tingley lost his son in such a tragic and senseless act of terrorism.

So, today, the first name that should appear at the top of the list will be PFC Steven D. Tingley, from Ellington, Connecticut, and my wish for the Tingley family is that they know there are so many people who have not forgotten their son's sacrifice and that one former United States Air Force Officer will never forget.

I Still Remember…and always will.

Tingley, Steven D. USA, PFC, 10/23/1983, CT, Ellington, CT

Carlson, Randall A. USA MAJ 09/25/1982 CT Trumbull, CT

Reagan, David L. USMC CPL 09/30/1982 VA Virginia Beach, VA

Maxwell, Ben H. USA SSGT 04/18/1983 VA Appomattox, VA

McMaugh, Robert V. USMC CPL 04/18/1983 VA Manassas, VA

Salazar, Mark E. USA SSGT 04/18/1983 CA Pasadena, CA

Twine, Richard USA SFC 04/18/1983 UK Salop, UK

Losey, Donald George USMC 2LT 08/29/1983 NC Winston Salem, NC

Ortega, Alexander M. USMC SSGT 08/29/1983 NY Rochester, NY

Clark, Randy W. USMC LCPL 09/06/1983 WI Minong, WI

Valle, Pedro J. USMC CPL 09/06/1983 RP San Juan, RP

Soifert, Alan H. USMC SGT 10/14/1983 NH Nashua, NH

Ohler, Michael J. USMC CAPT 10/16/1983 NY Huntington, NY

Abbott, Terry W. USMC CPL 10/23/1983 OH New Richmond, OH

Alexander, Clemon S.USMC LCPL 10/23/1983 FL Monticello, FL

Allman, John R. USMC PFC 10/23/1983 NM Carlsbad NM

Arnold, Moses J. Jr.USMC CPL 10/23/1983 PA Philadelphia, PA

Bailey, Charles K. USMC PFC 10/23/1983 MD Berlin, MD

Baker, Nicholas USMC LCPL 10/23/1983 VA Alexandria, VA

Banks, Johansen USMC LCPL 10/23/1983 MI Detroit, MI

177

Barrett, Richard E. USMC LCPL 10/23/1983 VA Tappahanock, VA

Bates, Ronny K. USN HM1 10/23/1983 SC Aiken, SC

Battle, David L. USMC 1stSGT 10/23/1983 NC Hubert, NC

Baynard, James R. USMC LCPL 10/23/1983 VA Richmond, VA

Beamon, Jesse W. USN HN 10/23/1983 FL Haines City, FL

Belmer, Alvin. USMC GYSGT 10/23/1983 NC Jacksonville, NC

Bland, Stephen USMC PFC 10/23/1983 NC Midway Park, NC

Blankenship, Richard L.USMC SGT 10/23/1983 NC Hubert, NC

Blocker, John W. USMC LCPL 10/23/1983 FL Yulee, FL

Boccia, Joseph J. Jr. USMC CAPT 10/23/1983 NY Northport, NY

Bohannon, Leon Jr. USMC CPL 10/23/1983 NC Jacksonville, NC

Bohnet, John R. Jr. USMC SSGT 10/23/1983 TN Memphis, TN

Bonk, John J. Jr. USMC CPL 10/23/1983 PA Philadelphia, PA

Boulos, Jeffrey L. USMC LCPL 10/23/1983 NY Islip, NY

Bousum, David R. USMC CPL 10/23/1983 MI Fife Lake, MI

Boyett, John N. USMC 1stLT 10/23/1983 NC Camp Lejeune, NC

Brown, Anthony USMC CPL 10/23/1983 MI Detroit, MI

Brown, David W. USMC LCPL 10/23/1983 TX Conroe, TX

Buchanan, Bobby S. Jr.USMC LCPL 10/23/1983 NC Midway Park, NC

Buckmaster, John B. USMC CPL 10/23/1983 OH Vandalia, OH

Burley, William F. USMC PFC 10/23/1983 NJ Linden, NJ

Cain, Jimmy R. USN HN 10/23/1983 AL Birmington, AL

Callahan, Paul L. USMC CPL 10/23/1983 OH Lorain, OH

Camara, Mecot E. USMC SGT 10/23/1983 NC Jacksonville, NC

Campus, Bradley J. USMC PFC 10/23/1983 MA Lynn, MA

Ceasar, Johnnie D. USMC LCPL 10/23/1983 TX El Campo, TX

Cole, Marc L. USMC PFC 10/23/1983 OH Ludlow Falls, OH

Coleman, Marcus A. USA SP4 10/23/1983 TX Dallas, TX

Comas, Juan M. USMC PFC 10/23/1983 FL Hialeah, FL

Conley, Robert A USMC SGT 10/23/1983 FL Orlando, FL

Cook, Charles D. USMC CPL 10/23/1983 NC Advance, NC

Cooper, Curtis J. USMC LCPL 10/23/1983 PA North Wales, PA

Copeland, Johnny L. USMC LCPL 10/23/1983 NC Burlington, NC

Corcoran, Bert D. USMC CPL 10/23/1983 NY Katonah, NY

Cosner, David L. USMC LCPL 10/23/1983 WV Elkins, WV

Coulman, Kevin P. USMC SGT 10/23/1983 NY Seminary, NY

Croft, Brett A. USMC LCPL 10/23/1983 FL Lakeland, FL

Crudale, Rick R. USMC LCPL 10/23/1983 RI Warwick, RI

Custard, Kevin P. USMC LCPL 10/23/1983 MN Virginia, MN

Cyzick, Russell E. USMC LCPL 10/23/1983 WV Star City, WV

Davis, Andrew L. USMC MAJ 10/23/1983 NC Jacksonville, NC

Decker, Sidney James USMC PFC 10/23/1983 KY Clarkson, KY

Devlin, Michael J. USMC PFC 10/23/1983 MA Westwood, MA

Dibenedetto, Thomas A. USMC LCPL 10/23/1983 CT Mansfield Center, CT

Dorsey, Nathaniel G. USMC PVT 10/23/1983 MD Baltimore, MD

Douglass, Frederick B. USMC SGTMAJ 10/23/1983 MA Cataumet, MA

Dunnigan, Timothy J. USMC CPL 10/23/1983 WV Princeton, WV

Earle, Bryan L. USN HN 10/23/1983 OH Painsville, OH

Edwards, Roy L. USMC MSGT 10/23/1983 NC Camp Lejeune, NC

Elliot, William D. Jr. USN HM3 10/23/1983 PA Lancaster, PA

Ellison, Jesse USMC LCPL 10/23/1983 WI Soldiers Grove, WI

Estes, Danny R. USMC PFC 10/23/1983 IN Gary, IN

Estler, Sean F. USMC PFC 10/23/1983 NJ Kenall Park, NJ

Faulk, James E. USN HM3 10/23/1983 FL Panama City, FL

Fluegel, Richard A. USMC PFC 10/23/1983 PA Erie, PA

Forrester, Steven M. USMC CPL 10/23/1983 NC Jacksonville, NC

Foster, William B. Jr. USN HM3 10/23/1983 VA Richmond, VA

Fulcher, Michael D USMC CPL 10/23/1983 VA Madison Heights, VA

Fuller, Benjamin E USMC LCPL 10/23/1983 GA Duluth, GA

Fulton, Michael S. USMC LCPL 10/23/1983 TX Ft. Worth, TX

Gaines, William Jr. USMC CPL 10/23/1983 FL Port Charlotte, FL

Gallagher, Sean R. USMC LCPL 10/23/1983 MA N. Andover, MA

Gander, David B. USMC LCPL 10/23/1983 WI Milwaulkee, WI

Gangur, George M. USMC LCPL 10/23/1983 OH Cleveland, OH

Gann, Leland E. USMC SSGT 10/23/1983 NC Camp Lejeune, NC

Garcia, Randall J. USMC LCPL 10/23/1983 CA Modesto, CA

Garcia, Ronald J. USMC SSGT 10/23/1983 NC Jacksonville, NC

Gay, David D. USMC LCPL 10/23/1983 NC Harrisburg, IL

Ghumm, Harold D. USMC SSGT 10/23/1983 NC Jacksonville, NC

Gibbs, Warner Jr. USMC LCPL 10/23/1983 VA Portsmouth, VA

Giblin, Timothy R. USMC CPL 10/23/1983 RI N. Providence, RI

Gorchinski, Michael W. USN ETC 10/23/1983 IN Evansville, IN

Gordon, Richard J. USMC LCPL 10/23/1983 MA Somerville, MA

Gratton, Harold F. USMC LCPL 10/23/1983 NY Conoes, NY

Greaser, Robert B. USMC SGT 10/23/1983 PA Lansdale, PA

Green, Davin M. USMC LCPL 10/23/1983 MD Baltimore, MD

Hairston, Thomas A. USMC LCPL 10/23/1983 PA Philadelphia, PA

Haltiwanger, Freddie Jr. USMC SGT 10/23/1983 SC Little Mountain, SC

Hamilton, Virgil D.USMC LCPL 10/23/1983 KY Dayton, OH

Hanton, Gilbert USMC SGT 10/23/1983 DC Washington, DC

Hart, William USMC LCPL 10/23/1983 NC Jacksonville, NC

Haskell, Michael S. USMC CAPT 10/23/1983 NC Camp Lejeune, NC

Hastings, Michael A. USMC PFC 10/23/1983 DE Seaford, DE

Hein, Paul A. USMC CAPT 10/23/1983 NC Camp Lejeune, NC

Held, Douglas E. USMC LCPL 10/23/1983 NC Jacksonville, NC

Helms, Mark A. USMC PFC 10/23/1983 NE Dwight, NE

Henderson, Ferrandy D. USMC LCPL 10/23/1983 FL Tampa, FL

Hernandez, Matilde Jr. USMC MSGT 10/23/1983 NC Midway Park, NC

Hester, Stanley G. USMC CPL 10/23/1983 NC Raleigh, NC

Hildreth, Donald W. USMC GYSGT 10/23/1983 NC Sneads Ferry, NC

Holberton, Richard H. USMC SSGT 10/23/1983 SC Beaufort, SC

Holland, Robert S. USN HM3 10/23/1983 KY Gilbertsville, KY

Hollingshead, Bruce A. USMC LCPL 10/23/1983 OH Fairborn, OH

Holmes, Melvin D. USMC PFC 10/23/1983 IL Chicago, IL

Howard, Bruce L. USMC CPL 10/23/1983 ME Strong, ME

Hudson, John R. USN LT 10/23/1983 GA Riverdale, GA

Hudson, Terry L. USMC CPL 10/23/1983 AL Prichard, AL

Hue, Lyndon J. USMC LCPL 10/23/1983 LA Des Allemands, LA

Hukill, Maurice E. USMC 2ndLT 10/23/1983 NC Jacksonville, NC

Iacovino, Edward F. Jr. USMC LCPL 10/23/1983 RI Warwick, RI

Ingalls, John J. USMC PFC 10/23/1983 NY Interlaken, NY

Innocenzi, Paul G. III USMC WO1 10/23/1983 NJ Trenton, NJ

Jackowski, James J. USMC CPL 10/23/1983 NY S. Salem, NY

James, Jeffrey W. USMC LCPL 10/23/1983 MD Baltimore, MD

Jenkins, Nathaniel W. USMC LCPL 10/23/1983 FL Daytona Beach, FL

Johnson, Michael H. USN HM2 10/23/1983 MI Detroit, MI

Johnston, Edward A. USMC CPL 10/23/1983 OH Struthers, OH

Jones, Steven USMC LCPL 10/23/1983 NY Brooklyn, NY

Julian, Thomas A. USMC PFC 10/23/1983 RI Middleton, RI

Kees, Marion E. USN HM2 10/23/1983 WV Martinsburg, WV

Keown, Thomas C. USMC SGT 10/23/1983 KY Louisville, KY

Kimm, Edward E. USMC GYSGT 10/23/1983 IA Atlantic, IA

Kingsley, Walter V. USMC LCPL 10/23/1983 WI Wisconsin Dells, WI

Kluck, Daniel S. USA SGT 10/23/1983 KY Owensboro, KY

Knipple, James C. USMC LCPL 10/23/1983 VA Alexandria, VA

Kreischer, Freas H. III USMC LCPL 10/23/1983 FL Indiatlantic, FL

Laise, Keith J. USMC LCPL 10/23/1983 PA East Stroudsburg, PA

Lamb, Thomas G. USMC LCPL 10/23/1983 MN Coon Rapids, MN

Langon, James J. IV USMC LCPL 10/23/1983 NJ Lakehurst, NJ

Lariviere, Michael S. USMC SGT 10/23/1983 FL Perry, FL

Lariviere, Steven B. USMC CPL 10/23/1983 MA Chicopee, MA

Lemnah, Richard L. USMC MSGT 10/23/1983 NC Camp Lejeune, NC

Lewis, David A. USMC CPL 10/23/1983 OH Garfield Heights, OH

Lewis, Val S. USMC SGT 10/23/1983 GA Atlanta, GA

Livingston, Joseph R. USMC CPL 10/23/1983 IL Champaign, IL

Lyon, Paul D. Jr. USMC LCPL 10/23/1983 FL Milton, FL

Macroglou, John W. USMC MAJ 10/23/1983 NC Jacksonville, NC

Maitland, Samuel USMC CPL 10/23/1983 NC Jacksonville, NC

Martin, Charlie R. USMC SSGT 10/23/1983 NC Camp Lejeune, NC

Martin, Jack L. USMC PFC 10/23/1983 FL Oveido, FL

Massa, David S. USMC CPL 10/23/1983 RI Warren, RI

Massman, Michael R. USMC SGT 10/23/1983 MI Port Huron, MI

Mattacchione, Joseph J. USMC PVT 10/23/1983 NC Sanford, NC

McCall, John USMC LCPL 10/23/1983 NY Rochester, NY

McDonough, James E. USMC SGT 10/23/1983 PA Newcastle, PA

McMahon, Timothy R. USMC LCPL 10/23/1983 TX Austin, TX

McNeely, Timothy D. USMC LCPL 10/23/1983NC Mooresville, NC

McVicker, George N. II USN HM2 10/23/1983 IN Wabash, IN

Melendez, Louis USMC PFC 10/23/1983 PR Puerto Rico

Menkins, Richard H. II USMC SGT 10/23/1983 NY Tully, NY

Mercer, Michael D. USMC CPL 10/23/1983 NC Vale, NC

Meurer, Ronald W. USMC LCPL 10/23/1983 NC Jacksonville, NC

Milano, Joseph P. USN HM3 10/23/1983 NY Farmingville, NY

Moore, Joseph P. USMC CPL 10/23/1983 MO St. Louis, MO

Morrow, Richard A. USMC LCPL 10/23/1983 PA Clairton, PA

Muffler, John F. USMC LCPL 10/23/1983 PA Philadelphia, PA

Munoz, Alex USMC CPL 10/23/1983 NM Bloomfield, NM

Myers, Harry D. USMC CPL 10/23/1983 NC Whittler, NC

Nairn, David J. USMC 1stLT 10/23/1983 NC Jacksonville, NC

Nava, Luis A. USMC LCPL 10/23/1983 CA Gardena, CA

Olson, John A. USMC CPL 10/23/1983 MN Sabin, MN

Olson, Robert P. USMC PFC 10/23/1983 NY Lawtons, NY

Ortiz, Richard C. USMC CWO3 10/23/1983 OK Ft. Sill, OK

Owen, Jeffrey B. USMC PFC 10/23/1983 VA Virginia Beach, VA

Owens, Joseph A. USMC CPL 10/23/1983 VA Chesterfield, VA

Page, Connie Ray USMC CPL 10/23/1983 NC Erwin, NC

Parker, Ulysses USMC LCPL 10/23/1983 MD Baltimore, MD

Payne, Mark W. USMC LCPL 10/23/1983 NY Binghamton, NY

Pearson, John L. USMC GYSGT 10/23/1983 NC Jacksonville, NC

Perron, Thomas S. USMC PFC 10/23/1983 MA Whitinsville, MA

Phillips, John A. Jr. USMC SGT 10/23/1983 IL Wilmette, IL

Piercy, George W. USN HMC 10/23/1983 MD Mt. Savage, MD

Plymel, Clyde W. USMC 1stLT 10/23/1983 FL Merritt, FL

Pollard, William H. USMC SGT 10/23/1983 NC Jacksonville, NC

Pomalestorres, Rafael I. USMC SGT 10/23/1983 PA Philadelphia, PA

Prevatt, Victor M. USMC CPL 10/23/1983 GA Columbus, GA

Price, James C. USMC PFC 10/23/1983 AL Attala, AL

Prindeville, Patrick K. USMC SSGT 10/23/1983 FL Gainesville, FL

Pulliam, Eric A. USMC PFC 10/23/1983 IL E. St. Louis, IL

Quirante, Diomedes J. USN HM3 10/23/1983 RP Calcoocan City, RP

Randolph, David M. USMC LCPL 10/23/1983 AZ Siloam Springs, AZ

Ray, Charles R. USMC GYSGT 10/23/1983 NC Jacksonville, NC

Relvas, Rui A. USMC PFC 10/23/1983 PA Philadelphia, PA

Rich, Terrence L. USMC PFC 10/23/1983 NY Brooklyn, NY

Richardson, Warren USMC LCPL 10/23/1983 NY Brooklyn, NY

Rodriguez, Juan C. USMC SGT 10/23/1983 FL Miami, FL

Rotondo, Louis J. USMC LCPL 10/23/1983 PA Philadelphia, PA

Sanpedro, Guillermo Jr. USMC LCPL 10/23/1983 FL Hialeah, FL

Sauls, Michael C. USMC LCPL 10/23/1983 SC Waterboro, SC

Schnorf, Charles J. USMC 1stLT 10/23/1983 NC Camp Lejeune, NC

Schultz, Scott L. USMC PFC 10/23/1983 NY Keeseville, NY

Scialabba, Peter J. USMC CAPT 10/23/1983 NC Moorehead City, NC

Scott, Gary R. USMC CPL 10/23/1983 IL Rankin, IL

Shallo, Ronald L. USMC CPL 10/23/1983 NY Hudson, NY

Shipp, Thomas A. USMC CPL 10/23/1983 NC Jacksonville, NC

Shropshire, Jerryl D. USMC LCPL 10/23/1983 GA Macon, GA

Silvia, James F. USMC LCPL 10/23/1983 RI Portsmouth, RI

Sliwinski, Stanley J. USMC LCPL 10/23/1983 OH Niles, OH

Smith, Kirk H. USMC LCPL 10/23/1983 FL Miami, FL

Smith, Thomas G. USMC SSGT 10/23/1983 CT Middletown, CT

Smith, Vincent L. USMC CAPT 10/23/1983 NC Jacksonville, NC

Soares, Edward USMC LCPL 10/23/1983 RI Tiverton, RI

Sommerhof, William S. USMC 1stLT 10/23/1983 IL Springfield, IL

Spaulding, Michael C. USMC LCPL 10/23/1983 OH Akron, OH

Spearing, John W. USMC LCPL 10/23/1983 PA Lancaster, PA

Spencer, Stephen E. USMC LCPL 10/23/1983 RI Portsmouth, RI

Stelpflug, Bill J. USMC LCPL 10/23/1983 AL Auburn, AL

Stephens, Horace R. USMC LCPL 10/23/1983 MD Capitol Heights, MD

Stockton, Craig S. USMC PFC 10/23/1983 NY Rochester, NY

Stokes, Jeffrey G. USMC LCPL 10/23/1983 GA Waynesboro, GA

Stowe, Thomas D. USMC LCPL 10/23/1983 NC Jacksonville, NC

Sturghill, Eric D. USMC LCPL 10/23/1983 IL Chicago, IL

Sundar, Devon L. USMC LCPL 10/23/1983 CT Standford, CT

Surch, James F. Jr. USN LT 10/23/1983 CA Lompoc, CA

Thompson, Dennis A. USMC CPL 10/23/1983 NY Bronx, NY

Thorstad, Thomas P. USMC SSGT 10/23/1983 IN Chesterton, IN

Tishmack, John J. USMC LCPL 10/23/1983 MN Minneapolis, MN

Trahan, Lex D. USMC PVT 10/23/1983 LA Lafayette, LA

Vallone, Donald H. Jr. USMC PFC 10/23/1983 CA Palmdale, CA

Walker, Eric R. USMC CPL 10/23/1983 IL Chicago, IL

Walker, Leonard W. USMC CPL 10/23/1983 AL Dothan, AL

Washington, Eric G. USMC CPL 10/23/1983 VA Alexandria, VA

Weekes, Obrian USMC CPL 10/23/1983 NY Brooklyn, NY

Wells, Tandy W. USMC 1stSGT 10/23/1983 NC Jacksonville, NC

Wentworth, Steven B. USMC LCPL 10/23/1983 PA Reading, PA

Wesley, Allen D. USMC SGT 10/23/1983 PA Philadelphia, PA

West, Lloyd D. USMC GYSGT 10/23/1983 NC Jacksonville, NC

Weyl, John R. USMC SSGT 10/23/1983 NC Jacksonville, NC

Wherland, Burton D. Jr. USMC CPL 10/23/1983 NC Jacksonville, NC

Wigglesworth, Dwayne W. USMC LCPL 10/23/1983 CT Naugatuck, CT

Williams, Rodney J. USMC LCPL 10/23/1983 FL Opa Locka, FL

Williams, Scipio Jr. USMC GYSGT 10/23/1983 SC Charleston, SC

Williamson, Johnny A. USMC LCPL 10/23/1983 NC Asheboro, NC

Wint, Walter E. Jr. USMC CAPT 10/23/1983 PA Wilkes-Barre, PA

Winter, William E. USMC CAPT 10/23/1983 SC Fripp Island, SC

Wolfe, John E. USMC CPL 10/23/1983 AZ Phoenix, AZ

Woollett, Donald E. USMC 1stLT 10/23/1983 OK Barthesville, OK

Worley, David E. USN HM3 10/23/1983 MD Baltimore, MD

Wyche, Craig L. USMC PFC 10/23/1983 NY Jamaica, NY

Yarber, James G. USA SFC 10/23/1983 CA Vacaville, CA

Young, Jeffrey D. USMC SGT 10/23/1983 NJ Moorestown, NJ

Zimmerman, William A. USMC 1stLT 10/23/1983 MI Grand Haven, MI

****

Townsend, Henry Jr. USMC CPL 12/02/1983 AL Montgomery, AL

Biddle, Shannon D. USMC CPL 12/04/1983 AL Valley Head, AL

Cherman, Sam USMC CPL 12/04/1983 NY Queens, NY

Cox, Manuel A. USMC SGT 12/04/1983 NJ Union City, NJ

Daugherty, David L. USMC CPL 12/04/1983 OH Eastlake,OH

Evans, Thomas A. USMC CPL 12/04/1983 MT Conrad, MT

Hattaway, Jeffrey T. USMC PFC 12/04/1983 FL Pensacola, FL

Kraft, Todd A. USMC CPL 12/04/1983 ND Devilslake, ND

Lange, Mark A. USN LT 12/04/1983 MI Fraser, MI

Perkins, Marvin H. USMC CPL 12/04/1983 TN Franklin, TN

Gargano, Edward J. USMC CPL 01/08/1984 MA Quincy, MA

Dramis, George L. USMC LCPL 01/30/1984 NJ Cape May Court House, NJ

*Hernandez, Rodolfo USMC 01/30/1984 TX El Paso, TX
(see below footnote)

Butler, Alfred III USMC CAPT 02/09/1984 FL Cocoa Beach, FL

Wagner, Michael USN IS1 09/20/1984 NC Zebulon,, NC

Welch, Kenneth USA WO2 09/20/1984 MI Grand Rapids, MI

*Hendrickson, John USMC '-' 04/13/1990 - (see below footnote)

*Simpson, Larry H. Jr. USMC '-' 08/31/1992 -(see below footnote)

Hasenfus, Michael USA CPL 10/20/1984 MA Dedham, MA

Stethem, Robert D. USN SW2 06/15/1985 MD Waldorf, MD

Higgins, William R. USMC COL 07/06/1990 KY Louisville, KY

*Still checking on the following to confirm information:

PLEASE NOTE: The symbol ' - ' denotes unknown to this web author, and does not mean that the information is unknown to the Department of Defense.

*Rivers, Paul USMC CPL 10/23/1983 NY Brooklyn, NY

(Listed in article, but his name is not on DOD list, but was in a 2/84 "Leatherneck" magazine article list. Later, it was confirmed by several eye witnesses that he did in fact survive the blast and is living.)

*Hernandez, Rodolfo USMC 01/31/1984 DOD - NOT IN LEBANON EVENT (Although the DoD Graves database has him listed as not died in Lebanon, but he was wounded on 30 Jan 84 and died weeks later in Germany as a result of wounds. Some references list him as being wounded 30 Jan and others 31 Jan, but it is believed he died on 08 Feb 1984 in a German hospital.)

Hendrickson, John USMC - 04/13/1990 DOD - NOT IN LEBANON EVENT

Simpson, Larry H. Jr. USMC - 08/31/1992 DOD - NOT IN LEBANON EVENT (Last 3 on one database, but not on

DOD list as being in Lebanon)

I took the above information from the Beirut Memorial Website at htpp://www.beirut-memorial.org/ and I also wish to invite all readers to visit their website. It is my understanding that the family members of those Peacekeepers who gave their lives in Beirut have designed a postage stamp to honor those who served and died in Beirut, Lebanon.

At this point, it is beyond my comprehension that nearly 25 years will pass on October 23, 2008, and there is no stamp to honor those killed in Beirut, Lebanon, the very first terrorist attack against American servicemen abroad.

Please help raise awareness by contacting the US Postmaster General. Let him know that this stamp is long overdue.

****

Finally, again I would like to reiterate that all profits derived from "Locked in Time" will go to the Department of Veterans Affairs, Denver, Colorado, for the treatment of servicemen and servicewomen who have been diagnosed with Post-Traumatic Stress Disorder, (PTSD).